HARVARD CITY PLANNING STUDIES

I

AIRPORTS

LONDON: HUMPHREY MILFORD

OXFORD UNIVERSITY PRESS

WICHITA MUNICIPAL AIRPORT

AIRPORTS

THEIR LOCATION, ADMINISTRATION AND LEGAL BASIS

BY

HENRY V. HUBBARD, MILLER McCLINTOCK
AND FRANK B. WILLIAMS

ASSISTED BY

PAUL MAHONEY AND HOWARD K. MENHINICK

CAMBRIDGE
HARVARD UNIVERSITY PRESS
1930

Harvard University Press

THE HARVARD CITY PLANNING STUDIES

PREFACE TO THE SERIES

The increased recognition of civic responsibility for guiding and rationalizing urban and regional growth brought about the establishment in 1929 by Harvard University of the Graduate School of City Planning, with research as a principal function. The facts and conclusions developed in a series of special studies, each conducted by a leading expert, are to be published as THE HARVARD CITY PLANNING STUDIES, of which two or three volumes will appear each year. The University hopes to render substantial service to the communities of this country by thus laying before the public and those concerned in civic development — city officials, engineers, architects, landscape architects, planning consultants, realtors, lawyers, members of chambers of commerce — freshly gathered and carefully analyzed information, compressed into monographs appearing shortly after each investigation is brought to a conclusion. While research alone can never solve the complicated problems of civic growth, it can contribute constructively if the facts selected are vital and representative, and presented in a form facilitating actual application in the promotion of wholesome trends of community life.

The vast range of problems in this country to-day which research should assist in crystallizing has been suggested in OUR CITIES TO-DAY AND TO-MORROW, by Hubbard and Hubbard, published in 1929 by the Harvard University Press: indeed this book may be regarded as the precursor of and introduction to the present series of studies.

Of the monographs for 1930, Volume I, AIRPORTS, is devoted to an urgent and much discussed field of municipal activity. Volume II, BUILDING HEIGHT, BULK, AND FORM: HOW ZONING CAN BE USED AS A PROTECTION AGAINST UNECONOMIC TYPES OF BUILDINGS, will be slightly delayed by the untimely death of its author, George B. Ford, during his final revision of the complete manuscript. Volume III, NEIGHBORHOODS OF SMALL HOMES IN AMERICA AND ENGLAND: WHAT THE COMMUNITY,

THE DEVELOPER, AND THE HOME OWNER CAN AFFORD AS TO SPACE
AND DENSITY, by Robert Whitten and Thomas Adams, representing the
last of the 1930 investigations, will therefore appear coincidently with or
even before Volume II.

It is to be hoped that these Studies will awaken discussion and that
they will call forth suggestions as to other practicable lines of research.
To these the Harvard School of City Planning will be glad to give consideration in preparing its program of special studies for each ensuing year.

THEODORA KIMBALL HUBBARD
Editor of Research

HENRY V. HUBBARD
Chairman

HARVARD UNIVERSITY
  SCHOOL OF CITY PLANNING
    September 15, 1930

CONTENTS

THE AIRPORT IN THE CITY PLAN

AIRPORT ADMINISTRATION

CONTENTS

APPENDICES

LIST OF ILLUSTRATIONS

PREFACE

The rapid growth of air transportation in the United States has far outstripped the knowledge and experience which should be brought to bear in directing this growth. As was the case in the expansion of our cities and in the adaptation of our highways to use by automobiles, so now in the case of airports a great many important decisions are being made without sufficient thought, because there appears not to be time for sufficient thought. Our growth will not wait for the compilation of data or the training of experts. The question with which we are confronted is really, therefore, whether this haphazard growth shall be accepted as natural, or whether every reasonable help shall be given to those who must deal with it, so that they may handle it, if not ideally, at least as intelligently as possible.

It often happens at present, and it will presumably happen with increasing frequency in the near future, that committeemen, public officials, or other representatives of communities are faced with the immediate concrete problem of the airport. They have to decide whether their community needs an airport as a necessary part of its connection with the air transportation system of its vicinity and of the country; what kind of airport it needs; where within the region tributary to the community an approximately flat area of perhaps two hundred acres may most efficiently be placed; how it should be related to the other uses of the land; what it would cost to build and to maintain; how these funds may best be raised; and how this essential transportation activity may be regulated legally and efficiently for the best interests of the community as a whole.

The purpose of the three reports comprised in this volume is to help as far as may be toward arriving at reasoned and reasonable decisions in this new and vital problem. It is evident that, as the conditions and requirements vary with each city, so the decisions must vary. All that can be done, at least in the light of our present knowledge, is to state the important factors, some of which at least will occur in each individual problem, and to suggest how these factors are usually related and how their relative importance may be evaluated. Decisions may thus be arrived at which shall be firmly based on an intelligent weighing of all the important considerations, both local and general, in each individual case.

If the responsible person feels, as he well may, that he needs assistance in coming to this decision, he may also get from these reports some suggestion as to what sort of assistance to call in to supplement his efforts in those portions of his problem in which he, himself, is not competent.

The questions of the actual setting aside of an area for an airport, as a part of a transportation system, but also as a functional part of all the areas ministering to the efficiency and success of the community, are matters of city and regional planning, and are treated in the first report by Professor Henry V. Hubbard and Mr. Howard K. Menhinick.

The questions of the methods of financing the purchase and maintenance of the municipal airport, together with the methods of the public regulation of all airports, are matters of municipal administration, and are treated in the second report by Dr. Miller McClintock and Mr. Paul Mahoney.

The questions of the legal rights and duties of the community in relation to the airport, the basis of precedent on which these rights and duties are founded, and the trend of opinion as to what further duties should be assumed by the community in this field, are matters of law, and are treated in the third report by Frank B. Williams, Esq.

The sequence of these reports is purely arbitrary. It was chosen only because the writers felt that on the whole the reader would grasp the subject more readily if he began with familiar, concrete, and specific considerations, and advanced to matters more general and more abstract.

In order to have first-hand and more complete information and to be able to check and to understand the data through personal familiarity with the site and the circumstances, Mr. Paul Mahoney visited eighty-five airports (see map on page 134) during a period of two and a half months and thus acquired, we believe, much more valuable information than could have been obtained through any set of questionnaires sent broadcast through the mails. The arrangements for this airport tour were made from the office of the Harvard School of City Planning by Mr. Howard K. Menhinick.

The expenses of the field study and the major portion of the cost of preparation of the first two of these reports have been paid by the Milton Fund of Harvard University through a grant for Research in Municipal

Airports. The third report has been made possible by an appropriation from the Harvard School of City Planning.

We gratefully acknowledge the assistance of hundreds of airport and city officials, aeronautical engineers, and city planners, who spent many valuable hours in giving us the benefit of their experience. The names of many of these kind coöperators will be found listed in Appendix 3. Colonel Harry H. Blee, Director of Aeronautic Development of the Aeronautics Branch of the United States Department of Commerce, furnished much indispensable technical information, and valuable legal suggestions were received from Elmer McD. Kintz, Esq., of the Aeronautics Branch. Mr. A. Pendleton Taliaferro, Jr., Chief, Airport Section, gave us many valuable suggestions as to which airports were most likely to repay a visit and careful study. The Aeronautics Branch of the Department of Commerce is rendering every service which it can to aviation. Despite a small staff and an enormous number of demands, its representatives are giving cities valuable advice as to the selection and development of airport sites. Pressed as they are by the many requests for their services, these men cannot give to each city as much time as they might wish in order to familiarize themselves completely with all the local conditions and to weigh all the many local factors involved in setting aside a portion of the city for an airport.

In addition to Mr. William Bennett Munro, Professor of American History and Government, Harvard University, whose interest in new phases of municipal administration first led to the plan for a detailed study of municipal airport control, we are much indebted to Robert L. Hale, Esq., Assistant Professor of Legal Economics at Columbia University, and to Mr. Harry J. Freeman, Research Fellow in Law, New York University of Law, and Director of the Legal and Legislative Research Service of the Aeronautical Chamber of Commerce of America, for material and suggestions with relation to the law of aeronautics.

Air transport companies freely assisted us in the study. We especially appreciate the courtesy of the Colonial Air Transport and the Universal Aviation Corporation in extending the privileges of their lines, thus making it possible for our field representative, Mr. Paul Mahoney, to cover a substantial proportion of the itinerary by air.

We are grateful to our research secretary, Miss Dorothy S. Rolfe, for her constant interest and painstaking assistance throughout this study, to Mr. Bradford Williams for his thorough editorial assistance, and to Mrs. Helen E. Terkelsen for intelligent work on proof and index.

If this research serves in some small measure to make available to each of our many friends and co-workers the experience of all the others, we shall feel that perhaps we have made some slight return to all of those who have given and are giving so freely of their time and assistance to advance the cause of aviation.

H. V. H.

CAMBRIDGE, MASSACHUSETTS
September 15, 1930

THE AIRPORT IN THE CITY PLAN

By

HENRY VINCENT HUBBARD

Norton Professor of Regional Planning, Harvard University School of City Planning
Editor of *City Planning*

and

HOWARD K. MENHINICK

Instructor in City Planning, Harvard University School of City Planning

INTRODUCTION

THE airport is primarily a part of a transportation system, — a system very important in the present and future life of a town, because it connects the town with the world at large and links it to the general progress of the whole community. In this respect the airport is like a railroad station; and, just as has often formerly happened in the case of the railroad station, an ill-considered location of the airport may now bring with it the disadvantages — increasing as time goes on — of undue congestion in its vicinity, of interruption of traffic, and of all the ills coming from allotting civic areas to wrong purposes and juxtaposing incongruous uses.

The airport is also a functional area, taking its place among all the functional areas which go to make up the total lands occupied or controlled by the community. The location of an airport is thus a city planning problem which can be solved correctly only by considering all the lands tributary to the community, and by being sure that the location and distribution of airports are the best possible, not only from the point of view of air transportation, but also from the point of view of the greatest efficiency and the least mutual harm for all the community which shall result from devoting so considerable a portion of its area to one specific and exclusive purpose.

To come to a decision which may not later bring contempt rather than honor to its authors, all the various factors which are concerned in this specific decision should be set down and evaluated at their relative worth. This is not a thing which can be done mechanically. It is possible and desirable to have a list of the factors which may occur, so that nothing may be forgotten, but the relative values of these factors will differ in each individual case, and no standardized "score card" giving a general method of arriving at a specific decision will prove of any final value beyond the point of suggestion.

Neither can any community guide itself with safety by copying the present accomplished results in another community.[1] In this report we

[1] See Appendix 4, Airport Managers' Suggestions and Criticisms as to Conditions at Their Airports.

have, to be sure, set down some statistics as to existing airports through-out the United States. It should be borne in mind, however, that these airports in their size, in their construction, in their location, and in their cost have often been the result of immediate pressure, of insufficient thought, of accidental circumstance; and though they may serve to show what poor conditions may be tolerated in some cases, and what conditions are now considered excellent in other cases, they cannot by any system of tabulation or averages produce a standard which anyone may copy in approaching the solution of a new problem.[1]

A tremendous amount of experience and experiment in relation to the interior design of the airport, and its methods of construction and of upkeep, is now becoming available to the airport designer. This present report does not deal with this side of the question. It considers, so to speak, only the external relations of the airport, — it considers the air-port as a unit in its relation to other units in the city plan.

Plainly, the solution of this problem can be arrived at much more readily and more surely by someone already familiar with such consider-ations in general and with the city plan, present or to come, of the specific community in particular. It is evident that the location of an airport is a problem similar to the location of a park or of a major highway system, or to the determination of a zoning plan. It is a duty and responsibility of the community, which normally devolves upon the City Plan Com-mission or whatever the name of the official body may be that has been selected to put before the community these vastly important problems, to ascertain and to guide the desires of the community in regard to them, and to codify and record the decision of the community as a guide in turn to the coördination of all the specific uses of land for the individual purposes of its different owners.

All this is a task which requires a great deal of knowledge and skill. It cannot effectively be divided among several authorities. If, there-fore, in any community the City Plan Commission, as it stands, is not capable of bearing the whole of this burden, the procedure obviously should be not to set up some other body for this specific purpose, not to dissipate this inseparable problem among a number of existing authori-ties, but to see to it that the City Plan Commission shall be made capable of handling this matter as a part of its whole great responsibility toward the community.

[1] See Appendix 5, Agencies Reported as Concerned in the Selection of Airport Sites; and Appendix 6, Factors which were Reported as Determining the Selection of Airport Sites.

CHAPTER I

PHYSICAL CHARACTERISTICS OF SUITABLE AIRPORT SITES

Size

WHEN faced with the problem of setting aside from all the lands of a community the most suitable site or number of related sites for use for airport purposes, the first factor which anyone would naturally seek to determine would be the required size. This of course depends on the amount and kind of use. In the present report, we are concerned with the interior use and layout of the airport only in so far as this affects the size and the other exterior relations of the airport as a unit in the city plan.

KINDS OF USE AFFECTING SIZE

The following kinds of use of the air are commonly found at airports in the United States:

1. Air mail
2. Transport
3. Schools
4. Air taxi service
5. Sight-seeing and joy riding
6. Use by private planes
7. Testing

The requirements of these uses as to character of ground surface are similar, although of course the ground requirements are different according as the air traffic is by landplane, by seaplane, or by dirigible.

Out of 80 airports furnishing information in this respect, there were 42 fields from which air mail was handled; 46 fields concerned in transport; 69 fields in which there was a school, — that is to say, in most cases merely an opportunity for instruction in flying; 67 fields from which planes were used for taxi service and sight-seeing and for joy riding, these uses not being capable of further separation; 64 fields which provided storage facilities for private planes, all 80 providing them with landing facilities; and 34 fields where airplane testing was carried on. All these uses are desirable, and at the present early stage in the development of airports it is to be expected that they will frequently occur together on the same field. It is plain, however, that as the use of the air

5

becomes more and more organized, some of these uses will be relegated to separate fields, and that therefore in selecting the desirable site of a municipal airport, for instance, it may not be necessary to consider that all these activities will take place within the area of this one port.

Air mail and transport are of course legitimate and permanent uses for the airport, in which the community is primarily interested. Testing of airplanes and instruction in flying are subsidiary activities which obviously are inconvenient and sometimes dangerous to the air mail and to transport if carried on in the same area at the same time. Separation of the instruction from the other activities of the airport by putting the school on a separate but adjoining field, as is planned at Columbus, Ohio, removes some of the ground dangers but does not completely eliminate the air hazards. Taxi service, sight-seeing and joy riding, and the use of private planes — if regulated as to the competence of the pilots, the efficiency of the planes, and obedience to the rules of the airport — would not be a detriment to the air mail and transport planes until the total amount of all these uses had increased to a point beyond the capacity of the airport. When this point is reached, it would seem that the private planes and the taxi-planes should be wholly or in part relegated to other fields, leaving the central or most important airport to handle the air mail and the transport.

RUNWAY DIMENSIONS RECOMMENDED BY DEPARTMENT OF COMMERCE

In considering the size of land ports, the Aeronautics Branch of the United States Department of Commerce has stated in Aeronautics Bulletin Number 16, "Airport Rating Regulations," that to secure a "1" rating on size of effective landing area, an airport must meet the following requirements:

> In addition to the basic requirements, an airport receiving a "1" rating on size of effective landing area shall have at least 2500 feet of effective landing area in all directions, with clear approaches, and the field shall be in good condition for landing at all times; or it shall have landing strips not less than 500 feet wide, permitting landing in at least eight directions at all times, the landing strips not to cross or converge at angles of less than 40°, nor any one of the landing strips to be less than 2500 feet in effective length, with clear approaches.

>   .   .   .   .

> When the airport lies at an altitude in excess of 1000 feet above sea level, the dimensions of the effective landing area or the effective

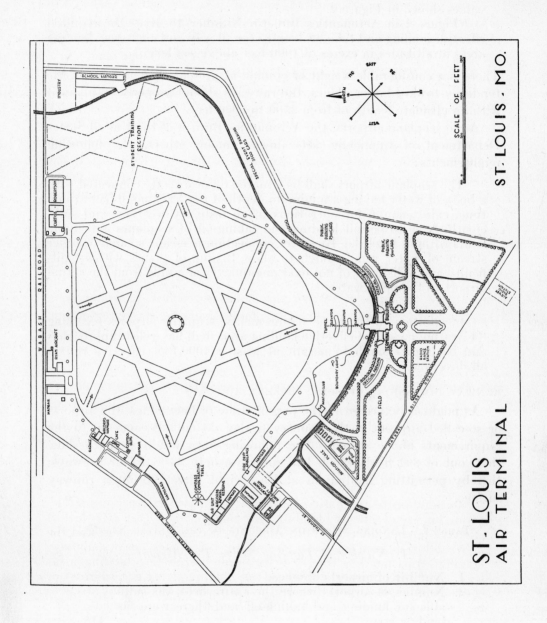

lengths of the landing strips shall be increased to the corresponding values shown in Figure 2.

(Figure 2 in Aeronautics Bulletin Number 16 gives the required effective landing and take-off lengths for all-way and eight-way landing areas at altitudes in excess of 1000 feet above sea level.)

There is a considerable weight of opinion at present that, in view of the tendency toward larger planes, the runways should properly be planned with an ultimate length of from 3500 to 5000 feet.

As to seaplane airports, the Aeronautics Branch of the United States Department of Commerce sets down, among others, the following requirements:

The seaplane airport shall be situated on or directly connected with a body of water having a minimum depth of not less than 6 feet at any time, calm enough for operations in all ordinary weather, and sufficiently large to permit landing and taking-off of seaplanes and flying boats without hazard. By direct connection is meant a canal or other stream of water wide enough to allow taxiing of planes without difficulty and a distance of not over one-quarter of a mile from the actual airport to the open water.

.   .   .   .

In addition to the basic requirements, seaplane airports receiving "1" rating on size of effective landing area shall have clear approaches and be large enough to permit at least a 4000-foot effective run in all directions.

RUNWAY DIMENSIONS OF SOME PRESENT AIRPORTS

As might be expected in the present time of beginnings, the airports or so-called airports in the country to-day do not all come up to the requirements above stated. The following data would seem to show that, out of 392 fields which had runways, only 33 had four runways, thereby permitting landing in at least eight directions on a runway surface.

TABLE I.   LANDING STRIPS ON AIRPORTS IN THE UNITED STATES [1]

A. *Number of Landing Strips Per Airport*

1. Number of airports observed 807
2. Number of airports where the entire field was suitable for landing and taking-off and there were no landing strips 415

[1] Data from Airway Bulletins of the Aeronautics Branch of the Department of Commerce through April, 1930.

3. Number of airports where the entire field was suitable for landing and taking-off but there were also landing strips 127
4. Number of airports possessing one landing strip . .   65
5. Number of airports possessing two landing strips . 238
6. Number of airports possessing three landing strips .   56
7. Number of airports possessing four landing strips .   33
8. Number of airports possessing more than four landing strips   0

B. *Number of Landing Strips of Various Lengths*

Number of landing strips whose length was given . . 809

Length in Feet	Number of Landing Strips	Length in Feet	Number of Landing Strips
500– 999	19	4000–4499	14
1000–1499	112	4500–4999	8
1500–1999	209	5000–5499	6
2000–2499	190	5500–5999	3
2500–2999	179	6000–6499	2
3000–3499	44	6500–6999	1
3500–3999	21	7000–7499	1

C. *Number of Landing Strips or Runways of Various Widths*

Number of landing strips or runways whose width was given 667

Width in Feet	Number of Landing Strips or Runways	Width in Feet	Number of Landing Strips or Runways
0– 49	8	650–699	20
50– 99	31	700–749	7
100–149	109	750–799	0
150–199	72	800–849	7
200–249	81	850–899	4
250–299	15	900–949	6
300–349	127	950–999	1
350–399	9	1000	5
400–449	46	1020	1
450–499	15	1200	1
500–549	62	1250	1
550–599	0	1280	1
600–649	37	1500	1

All the landing strips do not come up to the desired standard in length, for out of 809 landing strips recorded, only 279 had a length of 2500 feet or more.   There were 19 landing strips less than 1000 feet in length and only 13 that were 5000 feet or more in length.

The same is true of width, for out of 667 runways or landing strips of various widths, 513 were less than 500 feet in width, there being 8 that were less than 50 feet in width; only 10 were 1000 feet or more in width, the widest being 1500 feet.

OTHER SPACE ALLOTMENTS

In addition to the essential provision of length and width for the landing and taking-off of planes, the following directly subsidiary uses will require allotment of space in accordance with their relative importance in each particular case: (1) *storage space for planes*, both occasional storage out of doors and regular storage in hangars — if the port provides for a dirigible, its hangar will be of course a major consideration; (2) *overhauling and supply buildings* for storage of commonly needed supplies and for the overhauling and repairing of planes;   (3) *buildings for passengers and personnel*, giving at any rate waiting facilities and shelter, perhaps even hotel accommodations and a club room;   (4) *accessory buildings* for fire protection, general policing of the field, and for other uses;   (5) *area for the parking of the automobiles* of those coming to the field either as passengers or as spectators, particularly on special occasions.[1]   This last-mentioned area should be a differentiated part of the airport, or it may be immediately adjacent to the airport and under sufficient control by the management.   Some maintain that there should be 5 acres of parking space adjacent to the airport for every 100 planes that use the airport.   Suburban airports should make provision for commuters' automobiles to be left all day as is done near suburban railroad stations.

The actual size of the area which must be provided will be a thing for individual calculation in each case, according to the total demands of the uses just discussed.[2]   It is evident, however, that space may be saved by efficient and compact design, and that the absence of any obstacles in the immediate surroundings will avoid waste of land by the airport itself in securing the safety of planes approaching and leaving the field.

[1] See Appendix 7, Number of People Who Come to the Airport.
[2] See Appendix 8, Reported Daily Activity at Airports Visited.

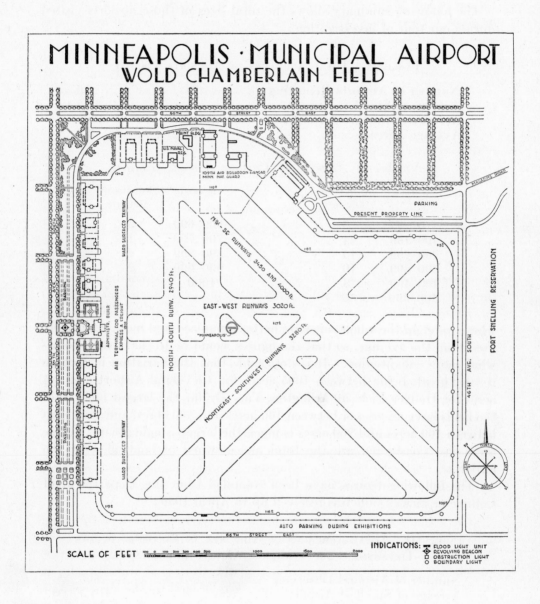

MINNEAPOLIS · MUNICIPAL AIRPORT
WOLD CHAMBERLAIN FIELD

SIZES OF SOME PRESENT AIRPORTS

The following summary shows the total sizes of those airports visited during our tour of investigation:

TABLE II.   TOTAL ACREAGES OF AIRPORTS VISITED

Number of Airports Reporting 76
Acreage of Smallest Airport 38.5
Acreage of Largest Airport. 1085
Average Acreage 338

Number of Airports in Various Acreage Groups

ACREAGE	NUMBER OF AIRPORTS	ACREAGE	NUMBER OF AIRPORTS
0– 99	3	600–699	3
100–199	24	700–799	1
200–299	15	800–899	2
300–399	10	900–999	2
400–499	8	1000+	2
500–599	6		

These were, on the whole, airports better organized and more intensively used than the average, so that the figures would be to that extent somewhat more enlightening. It is noticeable that the variation in acreage is very great, being between 1085 acres for Cleveland Airport and 38½ acres for Hoover Field at Arlington, Va. By far the largest number of the fields have an area of between 100 acres and 500 acres, and the group between 100 acres and 200 acres is much the largest single group. These areas just considered are the total areas owned or controlled by the airports.[1]

The following figures have been compiled from the Department of Commerce airway bulletins received up to April, 1930:

TABLE III.   TOTAL ACREAGES OF AIRPORTS AS REPORTED IN THE DEPARTMENT OF COMMERCE AIRWAY BULLETINS

Number of Airports Observed 803
Acreage of Smallest Airport 4.5
Acreage of Largest Airport 1440

[1] See also Appendix 9, Square Feet of Total and Developed Areas of Airports for Which These Figures Were Given.

Number of Airports in Various Acreage Groups

ACREAGE	NUMBER OF AIRPORTS	ACREAGE	NUMBER OF AIRPORTS
0– 49	222	500–599	6
50– 99	270	600–699	14
100–199	212	700–799	0
200–299	52	800–899	1
300–399	17	900–999	0
400–499	7	1000+	2

It is evident that any conclusions as to the proper size of an airport should be drawn with great caution from any data, particularly any data of averages based on present conditions. The sizes of our present airports have depended in most cases less upon a calculated adaptation of area to use than upon actual conditions as to pieces of land cheaply obtainable or already owned, or chosen for the reason of present accessibility or present cheapness of development.[1]

PREDICTION OF FUTURE SIZE REQUIREMENTS

In determining the amount of land to be set aside by a city for an airport, one should remember that it is of course a provision for the future that is being made, which must be based upon an estimate of future requirements. The amount of recourse to the airport reasonably to be predicted will depend on the population of the community, on the airmindedness of this population, and on the kind of activities normally carried on which would tend more or less in different cases to use of air transportation. It will depend also on the geographical relation of the town to air routes which will make airplane travel easy and effective or the reverse. It will depend on the future growth of air travel in regard to convenience and cheapness, a thing about which no one can make more than a guess, but no one could reasonably deny that the progress is bound to be very great indeed.

Perhaps here it should be said that it is unlikely that improvements in the ability of aircraft to alight and arise from the field will result in a reduction in the size of the field, because any such improvement would almost automatically bring about a completely offsetting increase in the number of aircraft.

Provision for future expansion is highly desirable. Some considerations which have been long since encountered in relation to parks apply

[1] See Appendix 6, Factors Which Were Reported as Determining the Selection of Airport Sites.

also to airports.   If more land is likely to be needed soon, it is better to get it at once while its price is low, rather than to raise the price first by the development of the airport.   This is perhaps less a factor with airports than with parks, because the park almost always raises immediately surrounding values, whereas there seems to be some evidence that the airport may depress them.   Again, as with parks, there is a size beyond which it is disadvantageous for the city to go in setting aside areas through which no streets may pass, and also there is probably a *sufficient* size for an airport, so that if the future use outgrows it, the answer would be not a *larger* airport but a differentiation of functions and *another* airport somewhere else.

SHAPE

An airport may have almost any shape, providing that suitably oriented and graded landing and take-off areas of sufficient length can be secured.   A reasonably compact shape has obvious advantages, but a large area with a smaller protruding portion, properly related, may be entirely satisfactory.   The prevailing winds may have an influence on the shape of the landing field by absolutely requiring an ample length in the direction of the winds, but sometimes allowing a minimum dimension across the winds, because so few landings take place in this direction. Similarly, any outside obstructions, natural or artificial, which tend to make one direction of approach very much more important than others, may have an effect upon the shape of the field.

The plans accompanying this report show some of the shapes of airports now operating with reasonable efficiency in the United States, and would seem to indicate that no standard of shape as yet exists.   Ideally, of course, a landing field should contain a circle, or perhaps some other compact figure, such as a triangle, capable of containing, in the eight primary compass directions, the longest required runways, thus allowing landing and departure in practically any direction.   The shape of the total field which includes the area for landing would then be determined by local possibilities and by the best arrangement of the various facilities auxiliary to flying.

ORIENTATION

Considerations of orientation apply almost exclusively to the direction of landing and taking-off of the planes.   If the field is amply large, this question is solved at once, since a plane may approach or leave the

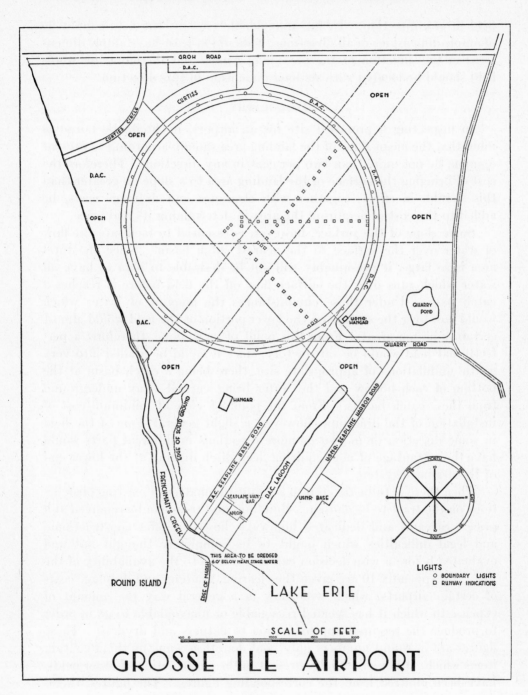

GROSSE ILE AIRPORT

field in any direction. If, for unavoidable reasons, the field cannot be of ample dimensions in all directions, it should at least have ample dimensions in the direction of the prevailing winds, and therefore the whole field should be located with its long dimension in this direction.

TOPOGRAPHY

In inspecting a proposed site for an airport, it should be borne in mind that the mean slope of the landing area should, according to present opinion, be not more than two per cent in any direction. Therefore the cost of bringing the surface of the landing area to a slope no greater than this should, in effect, together with clearance and drainage costs, be added to the cost of acquiring the area in determining its real price.

Some slope of the surface, however, is essential to facilitate the flow of water over the surface to the nearest catch basin. Since the total area is so large, it presumably will not be desirable to plan to have all water which runs over the surface flow off the field before it reaches a catch basin. Under those circumstances the amount of water which would flow over the surface on the lower portion of the field would almost certainly be too great. From this point of view alone, therefore, a perfectly flat field would be satisfactory, since it could be graded into very gentle undulations of appropriate size, there being a catch basin at the bottom of each hollow and the water being carried away underground from these catch basins. From the point of view of minimum cost of installation of the drainpipe, however, a slight general slope of the field in some direction or in two or more directions in different parts would have the advantage of not requiring deep ditch digging at the lower end of the drainage system.

Then there is to be taken into account the matter of existing obstructions on the tract to be chosen. Buildings and trees can be removed at a price. Streams and dedicated highways, however, offer constructional and legal difficulties which ought to be completely thought out and evaluated before a wise decision can be made as to the availability of the site. In Appendix 10 are given the clearing, grading, and drainage costs of certain airports, which will show in a general way the amount of expense to which it has seemed reasonable or unavoidable to go in order to produce the required approximation to flatness and dryness. These figures are in round numbers only, and doubtless some of them contain items which, although actually present in the construction of other fields, have been omitted from the corresponding figures. The figures, therefore, are not to be interpreted too literally, but since they depend so greatly on local conditions, the general conception which may be obtained from them is probably as valuable as something more specific would be, short of a really complete statement of the experience of one airport for the use of another airport under similar conditions.

Soil

In investigating the soil on a proposed site for an airport, four considerations are important: ease of excavation, firmness, porousness to facilitate surface and subsurface drainage, and fertility of the topsoil if areas are to be kept in turf. The drainage costs given in Appendix 10 show the dollars and cents value of a porous subsoil which would avoid the necessity of any considerable construction for soil drainage.

If any portion of the field on which airplanes are to land is to be covered with turf, then the topsoil must be fertile enough to support this turf with proper subsequent care, and it must also be porous enough to allow the water to sink down through it and not stand upon it for any length of time after a rain. It must be firm enough so that the wheels of a landing airplane will not sink into it appreciably, even when the soil is wet. If the surface on which the planes are to land is to be covered with concrete or some form of asphalt-bound pavement or similar surface, then the requirement of the subsoil is, of course, merely sufficient stability and sufficient porosity.

Atmospheric Conditions

In one way, the most important of all considerations in determining the excellence of a site for an airport is the question of the local atmospheric conditions which will help or hinder the maneuvering of planes in the air in its immediate vicinity. Rainfall, at least, is practically uniform throughout the whole region in which the airport must be located, and therefore will not operate to make one airport site within this region better than another. But to a surprising degree other atmospheric conditions differ locally within short distances, and in fact one site may be in this respect much superior to another not far away.

The direction and velocity of the wind are to be taken into account in their relation to the line of approach to the field and the local conditions of landing. Particularly are to be considered the predictability and constancy of the wind. Obviously an airport so located in relation to adjoining hills that it is subject to unpredictable air currents and eddies will be an undesirable field.

The clearness of the atmosphere is an important consideration. There should be as little fog as possible, and in a region where some fog is inevitable, the field should be so located that the prevailing winds will blow the fog away from the airport rather than toward it, and so that when there is only a slight current of air, the fog will tend to drain naturally away from the airport.

Similarly in regard to the obscuring of the air by smoke, if there are factories, etc., producing smoke, the airport should be located so that the prevailing winds blow the smoke away from the airport.   And again, the airport would presumably be better upon a slight elevation of ground so that the smoke would tend to flow away from the airport rather than to settle over it.

The amount of rainfall is an essential question but, as we have said, it will seldom have much influence in the decision between the availability of one site and another site in the same region.   Similarly as to snowfall, the actual amount of precipitation of snow would probably be fairly constant throughout a region, but the relation of each individual site to the prevailing wind and to surrounding obstructions to the wind, and therefore to the exact way in which the snow would drift and accumulate, is a very important consideration where the question of snowfall enters into the problem at all.

Physical Characteristics of the Surroundings

In a general way it may be said that an airplane on leaving a field can be depended on to rise after it has taken the air at a rate of one foot vertically for every seven feet traversed horizontally.   The surroundings of the airport therefore should be such that no obstructions extend upward into the space through any part of which a plane so rising might travel.   Of course this applies not only to buildings and other solid and bulky structures and to trees and chimneys, but equally and perhaps with added force to constructions like power lines, radio masts, etc., which offer the added danger of being less easy to see.   Where nothing better can be done, some obstructions rising above the specified line might be tolerated if they lie in a direction in which airplanes would practically never go.   But obstructions are always objectionable, and their presence should be avoided if this is in any way possible.

There are obvious advantages, both in ease of seeing the airport from a distance and certainty of freedom from all obstructions, if the surrounding country lies lower than the airport.   We have already mentioned the fact that higher land surrounding an airport is likely to be undesirable, both because the airplane must make a longer rise to clear it and because of the possible atmospheric difficulties of peculiar air currents, fog and smoke,[1] and the possible drainage difficulties of surface water flowing onto the airport itself.

[1] See Appendix 11, Difficulties Due to Developments in Surrounding Areas.

CHAPTER II

FUNCTIONAL RELATION OF THE AIRPORT TO THE CITY AND REGION

IN addition to the various local and specific considerations which we have already discussed, there are factors of broader relation which vitally affect the choice of a site for an airport. One is the relation of the airport, or of a number of airports serving the same region, to all the other areas in the region which, taken together, the community hopes to organize into one efficient whole, each area serving its best purpose. In other words, the location of the airport should be considered in relation to a consistent city and regional plan.

The function of the airport in the city plan is, as we have said, that of a part of a great transportation agency. We have seen that in these early days of air transport many airports are being used in a rather undifferentiated way for various kinds of air transportation and for many different auxiliary purposes. Undoubtedly, however, it will soon become necessary to segregate these uses and to have different airports for different purposes. We do not believe that anyone can predict with certainty at this time what will be the typical provision of differentiated airports which will serve the city of the future. Judging, however, from such knowledge of conditions and tendencies as we now have, we believe that the following kind of differentiation and arrangement is not improbable as a complete provision for a large city and its tributary region.

POSSIBLE REGIONAL SYSTEM OF AIRPORTS

INTOWN MUNICIPAL AIRPORT

First, the city might have a large intown municipal airport, which would be to air transportation what a union railroad station is to a railroad system. This airport should be as near the center of the town as possible. A greater transportation time than fifteen minutes from the center of the city to the airport would in all probability be a serious detriment. It should be noted that this is fifteen minutes' transportation

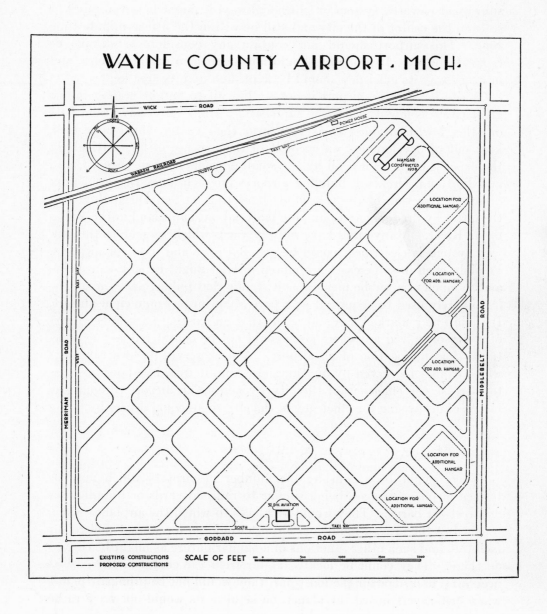

time by any available means, and if the airport were served by a good subway or elevated system or super-highway, it might lie seven miles or so from the center of the city and still be within the fifteen-minute time zone. This airport should not contain any considerable storage or repair facilities. It probably should not be open to private planes, and in every way its efficiency should be kept high and its area kept low.

A site for such an airport is not so difficult to find at present in our great cities as might at first be supposed.[1] Many cities have tidal flats or other low, undrained areas very near their center which have been kept out of development on account of the expense of fill, particularly the expense of piecemeal fill by the small developer. San Diego, Calif., and Portland, Ore., are building airports on such sites, the former by dredging a section of the tide lands bordering on San Diego Bay, and the latter by dredging and pumping material onto an island in the Willamette River. Many cities have railway yards which, as soon as the railway system is electrified, could be covered over and used for airports. Possibly even in some cases a blighted district might be so low in value and so much of a public menace as it stands that public money might be legitimately used to acquire it as a part of an intown municipal airport. It should be remarked here, however, that an existing park in the heart of a city or indeed anywhere else should not be considered as an opportunity for the location of an airport. A park serves its own functions which cannot be served by anything else, and it would be poor business to increase the efficiency of the city by adding an airport through the means of decreasing the efficiency of the city to an equal degree by losing a park.

AIRPLANE STORAGE AND REPAIR FIELDS

There might be a considerable number of airports which may be termed airplane garages, being similar to railroad yards or roundhouses or street-car barns. They would be places to which the airplanes which touched at the intown municipal airport would go for storage and repair facilities, and such other functions of a similar nature as might be carried on there. They could be located as far from the center of the city as necessary, and since for the most part they would not be primarily places where passengers board the planes, these airports would not have to be so closely related to the ground transportation system of the community.

[1] See Appendix 12, Areas within a Twenty-minute Radius of the Heart of the City by Present Means of Transportation Which Are Still Available for Airport Sites.

AIRPLANE PARKING FIELDS

There might be an outer circle of airports on the analogy of parking spaces and garages at the outer termini of rapid transit systems; *i.e.*, these airports would be places to which the people residing in the suburbs or in the country could come by private airplane or taxi airplane, and from which they could be moved quickly by mass transportation facilities to the heart of the city. These airports would have to provide storage facilities primarily for private commuting planes.

LOCAL SUBURBAN AIRPORTS

Then there could be, located at suburban centers which might be a very considerable distance from the heart of the big city, local suburban airports which would be near the homes of a considerable body of the population and would be the airports used by this local population in going to and from the big city by air.

PRIVATE AND SPECIAL AIRPORTS

Also there would be various kinds of private airports; *i.e.*, landing fields for airplane clubs, manufacturers' testing fields, and so on. It is not difficult to think of other specific uses which might make the construction of a special airport reasonable. For instance, a large area for recreation purposes, otherwise inaccessible, might be made many times more valuable by a special airport.

It has been frequently recommended that intermediate landing fields, perhaps not more than ten miles apart or even closer, should be constructed primarily as a safety provision along the main routes of air travel. The fact that they could serve this purpose also will doubtless hasten the construction of a considerable number of local airports primarily for local purposes.

It should be borne in mind, however, in considering this or any other scheme for the distribution and location of airports, that the airport like the park should be a continuous area, not cut through by public roads, and therefore it is bound to be, on account of its size, an interruption to public traffic on the ground. It might be said that if a park already exists, a location for an airport directly beyond the park from the center of the city or directly between the park and the center of the city would have the advantage of not diverting radial traffic any more than this has already been inevitably diverted by the park. Therefore it is essential, in relating the airports to the regional plan, that they be considered together with the main highway system, so that they shall be accessible by highway but shall not interrupt main lines of traffic; and that they be considered in relation to the population, its kind, its location, and its density, so that they shall not interrupt residential or other areas which should be continuous, and of course so that they shall not unnecessarily occupy areas which would be more efficiently occupied by dwellings or other types of land use.

The considerations of drainage and sewerage are likely to prove very important. Many cities contain areas which could be filled and drained sufficiently to make entirely satisfactory airports, but from which, if they were occupied by a dense population, sanitary sewage could be collected and discharged only at a disproportionate cost.

Of course we do not expect that any such complete and differentiated system of airports as above discussed is likely to be constructed by any but a few of our greater cities in the immediate future, though it is interesting to note in this connection that at the present time the Columbus airport, Port Columbus, is surrounded by five smaller airports within a radius of five miles. In our further discussion, however, in speaking of the airport we shall have in mind rather the kind of airport that a city should provide at this time and which it would use for general purposes until such time as more specialization is justified.

RELATION OF THE AIRPORT TO VARIOUS MEANS OF TRANSPORTATION

AIRWAYS

The decision as to the location of the airport may be affected by the consideration of the relation of the airlines to be served by this port. If a main airway already exists, the proposed new airport would naturally be as nearly on this airway as possible, not only to save distance on the airway, but on account of the additional difficulties which arise in the handling of radio beacons and such direction-giving devices when there is a bend in the airway. Where possible the airport should be so located that the airways converging upon it lie over less densely developed and inhabited portions of the town. This lessens the annoyance to the citizens from noise, and from the danger, slight though it is in any case, of falling planes, and equally it lessens the danger to the plane and its pilot, since there is a better chance in the more open country of making an emergency landing; indeed intermediate emergency landing fields could be much more readily secured along such a route.

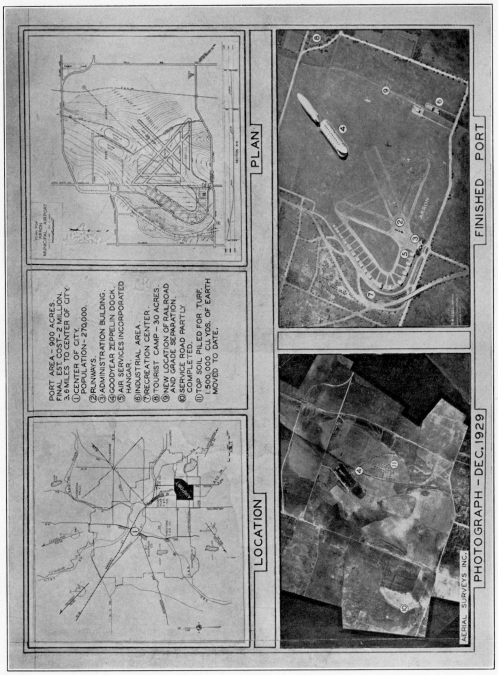

PLAN

LOCATION

PORT AREA – 900 ACRES.
FINAL EST. COST – 2 MILLION.
3.6 MILES TO CENTER OF CITY.
① CENTER OF CITY.
   POPULATION – 270,000.
② RUNWAYS.
③ ADMINISTRATION BUILDING.
④ GOODYEAR ZEPPELIN DOCK.
⑤ AIR SERVICES INCORPORATED
   HANGAR.
⑥ INDUSTRIAL AREA.
⑦ RECREATION CENTER.
⑧ TOURIST CAMP – 30 ACRES.
⑨ NEW LOCATION OF RAILROAD
   AND GRADE SEPARATION.
⑩ SERVICE ROAD PARTLY
   COMPLETED.
⑪ TOP SOIL PILED FOR TURF.
   1,500,000 CU. YDS. OF EARTH
   MOVED TO DATE.

FINISHED PORT

AERIAL SURVEYS INC.

PHOTOGRAPH – DEC. 1929

AKRON MUNICIPAL AIRPORT

Courtesy of Akron Airport Board

If both landplanes and seaplanes are using the airway, a port adjacent to a body of water which would permit the landing of seaplanes and possibly the transfer of passengers and cargo between landplane and seaplane at the port might be advantageously chosen. Although many opportunities for the use of water surfaces exist, very little development of this kind has taken place.[1]

The principal advantage of air transportation is that it saves time, but in order to make use of air transportation the passenger must get to the airport where he starts and get from the airport at which he arrives, and he might easily spend more time in this amount of land transportation than he spent in air transportation from one airport to another. The relation, therefore, of the airport to various kinds of land transport is very important indeed.

RAILROADS

A location directly on an important railroad line [2] is an advantage because it aids pilots in locating the airport since they can follow the railroad lines very readily. Also it facilitates the transfer of passengers and freight from plane to train and vice versa. Further, it is then easy to provide spur tracks for the shipment of oil, gasoline, and various other materials in large quantities to the airport. Indeed it might be said that no large airport could afford to be without at least a spur-line railroad connection; and where an airport is not located on an existing railroad line, the possibility of the construction of such a spur line should be carefully considered. If the airport were built directly over a railroad terminal or railroad yards, this connection between air and railway would be ideally provided.

TRANSIT

By proximity to the center of the city we mean, of course, proximity in time rather than proximity in space.[3] The better the transit facilities, the farther in miles the airport can be located from the center of the city. Other things being equal, the problem is to secure the greatest proximity

---

[1] See Appendix 13, Water Areas and Plans which have been Made to Use Them as Seaplane Bases.

[2] See Appendix 14, Airports at Various Distances from Nearest Steam Railroad Passenger Station on a Main Line; and Appendix 15, Airports at Various Distances from Nearest Freight Station on a Main Line.

[3] See Appendix 16, Airports and Transportation Time from Business Centers of Cities; and Appendix 17, Airports at Various Distances from Business Centers of Cities.

in point of time to the center of the city per dollar invested. In each case the authority locating an airport must determine whether the most per dollar can be obtained by purchasing physical nearness or by paying for transit facilities.[1]

Surface Car Lines. The presence of a surface car line would be a consideration affecting the location of an airport. But if this car line operated on a public street, it probably would be no better than a line of busses, and a line of busses could operate over any street which was wide enough and properly located. It is unlikely, therefore, that surface car lines would be built to airports primarily for the purpose of serving them, and usually an existing surface car line is not likely to be a governing element in the problem except in those cases where the car line is operating on an independent right of way and is really in effect a railroad.

Bus Lines. Bus transportation from the airport to the center of the city may be absolutely essential and presumably will be desirable in almost all cases. Airport-owned busses might at first be necessary to accommodate the airport traffic, being later superseded by general public service busses if the total traffic should become sufficient to show a profit for such a venture.[2] Since the bus line like the private automobile uses the public highway system, the question of bus transportation in its relation to airport location really comes down to a matter of a satisfactory highway system, which we shall discuss later.

Elevated and Subway Lines. Since an elevated line gives service that is much faster than ordinary surface transportation, and since the cost of building an elevated structure is so great, proximity to such a line already existing would be a very desirable feature in the location of an airport. The same thing may be said with even more force in regard to a subway. On the other hand, it should be remembered that an existing subway or an existing elevated line has been built because of an existing or immediately predictable traffic demand, and that land near such lines is already of high value, to say nothing of the inflated value due to speculation which very frequently is found also in such places.

HIGHWAYS

The relation of the airport to the main highway system cannot be neglected with impunity, no matter how important the other considerations may be. Its importance was illustrated in Atlanta, Ga. during an

---

[1] See Appendix 18, Transit Service to Airports.
[2] See Appendix 7, Number of People Who Come to the Airport.

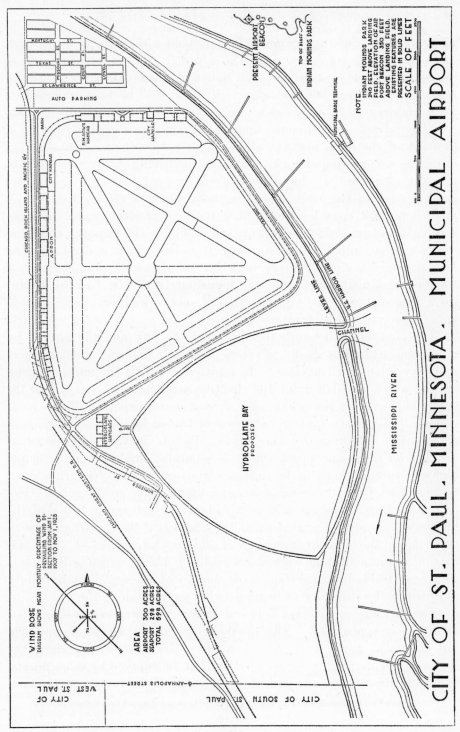

CITY OF ST. PAUL. MINNESOTA. MUNICIPAL AIRPORT

27

air meet when traffic was jammed for miles along the road to the airport, and many people could not reach the airport. The airport should be so related to the whole street network that access from all parts of the city is reasonably direct and unobstructed. It should be near enough to a main highway to be very easily accessible from it, but ideally the airport should not abut directly upon it for any considerable length. A location off the main highway eliminates the hazard and inconvenience of having cars parked along the highway or driving slowly to watch the airplane activities. It eliminates the real or mental hazard of airplanes passing close to the wires and the traffic along a crowded street. A more important consideration is that the land abutting upon the highway has frontage values, which are not assets to the airport as such, as long as it has sufficient access. Also it is frequently easier to control the surrounding development, both for safety and for appearance, if there is not a main public highway immediately abutting on the airport for a long distance, the opposite side of such a highway being high in value on account of its frontage.

The connection between the center of the city and the airport by automobile or by bus should, of course, be over a highway which is direct and expeditious for traveling.[1] In most cases this is the master consideration which will determine the effective nearness of the airport to the center of the city. For a long time at least, most airports will not create enough traffic to warrant an extension of transit facilities for their sake alone. The following are the obvious factors making for consistent rapidity for the connecting traffic: (1) separated grades at the principal highway intersections, as for instance the route from Newark airport to New York City; (2) elimination of railroad grade crossings; (3) freedom from ferry crossings and drawbridges; (4) adequate width of the highway; (5) proper pavement of the highway; (6) proper control of traffic along the highway, especially at all street intersections; (7) avoidance of a route through subcenters and any places which will cause a slowing of traffic by congestion, by frequency of crossing, by uncertainty of direction, by difficulty of turning, or by parking along the way.

The highway connection between airport and city center should be attractive in appearance. This should be true of any means of approach, but it applies particularly to the highway because beauty along the highway is more readily appreciated and can be enjoyed by more people. Out of 82 airports, 28 reported the appearance of the route as attractive,

---

[1] See Appendix 19, Impediments to Highway Travel between Airport and Center of City.

28 as fair, and 26 as unattractive. This consideration of appearance leads naturally to the suggestion that the approach to the airport should be by means of the "park system." In so far as the "park system" is a part of the transportation system, — that is, in so far as the suggestion contemplates carrying the traffic to and from the airport through boulevards and parkways, new or already existing, and does not contemplate the creating of new roads through existing parks, — this advantage should be obtained as far as possible. It will make a pleasant approach to the airport, which will have a definite value to the airport since a visit to it can form a part of a pleasure drive along the parkway.

Relation of the Airport to Other Functional Areas

Having considered the relation of the airport to the transportation system of the city, we shall now take up its relation to the different functional areas of the city: that is, such areas, present and predetermined, as would normally be demarcated on a zoning plan.

RELATION TO RESIDENTIAL DISTRICTS

The effect of the residential district upon the airport is not likely to be harmful except that tall apartment houses, school buildings, hospitals, or churches with spires, if located too near to the field, may be obstructions. This difficulty could easily be eliminated or minimized by forethought, both in the carrying out of a zoning plan and in the location of the landing field. Trees, however, are normal accompaniments of a residential district and occur so consistently throughout a district that any necessary avoidance of difficulty from this source will usually have to be done by the airport, so to speak, and not by any restriction of the district, though such restriction might be legal.[1]

As to the effect of the airport upon the district, the present consensus of opinion seems to be that in the following ways the airport is a detriment to residential values of the territory immediately adjacent to the port and to a lesser degree for a radius of perhaps one-half mile around the port.[2]

Noise.[3] This is particularly objectionable to hospitals and such institutions, but it must be to some extent a detriment to ordinary residential use, even though it may be said that people will get used to this noise just as they have become accustomed to many other new noises in the past.

[1] For further discussion of trees near the airport, see p. 129.
[2] See Appendix 20, Width of Annoyance Fringe around an Airport.
[3] See Appendix 21, Objections to Airports Made by Those Living in Their Vicinity.

The noise of the airplane engine may be largely overcome by improvements.   As far as we can now see, the noise of the propeller in the air will probably always remain.

Dust.[1]   Dust from the landing field has in the past been protested against as being a very considerable nuisance to a surrounding residential district.   Presumably, however, when airports are properly constructed and properly maintained, this nuisance will be abolished, and it is not likely to be tolerated for long, because it is a nuisance not only to the surrounding area, but in a greater degree to the airport itself.

Night Lighting.[1]   It has been said that the night lighting of the airport is a detriment to the surrounding region.   It would appear that most of these statements were made before the actual lighting was installed, and the difficulty proved to be less serious when the facts were definitely known.   Night lighting, if objectionable at all, is primarily objectionable only to residents on abutting property.   Moreover, a careful design of the different kinds of lights which are necessary at an airport will usually make it possible to avoid very much glare along the ground outside of the airport and still will leave the lighting entirely efficient from the point of view of the airport itself.

Danger.[1]   A good deal has been said about the danger to life and property caused by the proximity of an airport.   It cannot be denied that persons have been killed and property has been destroyed by the accidental falling of an airplane into a residential or other neighborhood. Presumably, no improvements in air navigation will entirely eliminate this risk.   But there is no reason to suppose that the risk will be any greater (if indeed it is now greater) than the risk which still remains to every citizen in crossing the street or, indeed, in going up and down stairs.   Even at present we are inclined to believe that any existing depreciation of surrounding values due to the fear of danger from falling airplanes is much more the result of a mental hazard than a practical hazard, and that the fear will disappear to a large degree as time proves that the danger is very slight.   Insurance covering property damage caused by falling aircraft and aircraft equipment is offered by some insurance companies, but they naturally have very little accumulated data on which to base their rates.   Therefore, these rates cannot now be used as a measure of the danger from falling aircraft.

Traffic Congestion.   It has been said that if the airport be approached through a residential district, the increased traffic, particularly on special

[1] See Appendix 21, Objections to Airports Made by Those Living in Their Vicinity.

occasions, will be detrimental to residential values, and the parking of the automobiles of visitors to the airport along the residential streets which should be quiet will be a distinct nuisance to the inhabitants. This doubtless will be true if provisions are not made to forestall it, but a proper relation of the airport to the main transportation system would prevent an unreasonable disproportion between the amount of traffic and the width of streets. A proper provision of parking facilities under the control of the airport itself would eliminate the necessity for promiscuous parking elsewhere.

Effect on Land Values. In determining whether on the whole the immediate presence of an airport is an advantage or a disadvantage to a residential district, the few figures which seem now to be available really do not prove any point on either side of the question.[1] In most cases where the construction of an airport has been said to raise values in a residential district, it has done so because the district was very sparsely settled and low in price per acre, and the presence of the airport by making opportunity for some local development, cheap residential or local commercial, did raise the value of some of the land immediately adjacent to the port. If an airport were to be located contiguous to a low-cost, densely populated residential district, still the airport might raise values slightly because, for the abutting dwellings, a view into the airport, for all its noises and lights, would be preferable to a view into a continuation of the same congested residential district. On the other hand, if an airport abuts on a higher-cost residential district, the balance is likely to turn the other way, and the abutting residences will lose in value instead of gaining by the presence of the airport.

At any rate, whatever the final facts may prove to be, there seems to be at present considerable feeling that an airport is not a thing to be sought in a residential district, for the sake of the residential district. Nevertheless, the airport cannot be excluded completely from all residential districts because this would be likely to render impossible the efficient location and operation of this essential municipal service.

RELATION TO COMMERCIAL DISTRICTS

As to the relation of an airport to a commercial district, the effect of the district upon the airport is disadvantageous in the following ways: it creates an approach hazard by its closely built character, its tall structures, the unpredictable air currents generated above it, and to some

[1] See Appendix 22, The Effect of the Airport on Land Values.

extent by the presence of smoke. Evidently some of these disadvantages would be minimized by locating the airport to windward of the center of the commercial district. The greatest argument against the location of the airport in a commercial district is, of course, the fact that the intensive use of the land in a commercial district causes such high land values that an adequate area for an airport would be likely to be prohibitively expensive.

As to the effect of the airport on a commercial district, there is the hazard of the approaching planes over an area where both population and values are highly concentrated, and there is the fact that the large expanse of the airport would create a barrier which might be a serious disadvantage to the ordinary expansion of business and access to the business area. Of course it should be borne in mind in connection with the intown location of an airport that the intown lands of a community are not of equal value, nor do they grade down consistently from high values in the center to low values on the outskirts. Considerable areas of low values are found for one reason or another close to the heart of the city, and therefore an airport might sometimes be built very near a central district but not in it. An example is the proposed airport on the Chicago water front.

As to local shopping districts, they are so small and the airport is so large that the relation between the two would presumably be merely that the airport would be located for more important reasons, and that the local shopping districts with their business structures would tend to cluster at the approaches of the airport.

RELATION TO INDUSTRIAL DISTRICTS

In the case of the relation of the airport to an industrial district, the effect of this district on the airport would be detrimental in the following ways: factory chimneys would constitute a hazard in themselves, and their smoke would also be a serious hazard. Also the heat and the generally unpredictable air currents to be found over such regions make flying more difficult and dangerous. The approaches and surroundings of an airport in an industrial district are likely, moreover, to be less appealing to the tastes of the people who would normally patronize air transport.

As to the effect of the airport upon the district, there is no reason to suppose that it would have any injurious effect, unless the presence of so large an uninterrupted area should bring about difficulties of transportation and difficulties of expansion which, to be sure, might prove very serious.

RELATION TO THE RECREATION SYSTEM

Here we should first of all remember that an airport is not a legitimate element of the public recreation system. Airplanes are primarily a means of transportation and not of recreation. The use of airplanes for recreation is limited to a very small fraction of the total population, and to a considerable extent the recreational use is dependent on novelty and will presumably decline as we all become more familiar with air travel, just as taking a ride in an automobile has ceased for all of us to be an adventure and for many of us to be a pleasure.

Recreational areas can properly offer to the airport little advantage, if due regard be paid to their own proper recreational function. They cannot be used as intermediate landing fields and remain parks. No man would be content to allow his children to play in a park into which an airplane might descend at any moment and for any unimportant reason. The occasional use of any available open area by an airplane in distress, which must make the best landing it can under the circumstances, is something to which no one can object and which after all would happen so seldom that its danger would be almost negligible, looked at from the point of view of any one individual's chance of being involved in it.

The location of a park system and the size and function of its constituent units are worked out in relation to the outdoor recreational needs of the population, in relation to the topography, and in relation to the park system's function as a part of a unified city plan. The only reason, therefore, which could possibly excuse the taking of park land for an airport would be the absolute demonstration that the land was not suitable for use as a park, or was not needed and could never be needed as a park. And it is very rare indeed that this can be said of the existing park holdings of any community in this country. The statistics [1] in regard to the use of park land for airports are likely to be misleading if it be not remembered that in many cases the community had the power to acquire land for parks by eminent domain, but did not have this power to acquire land for airports, specifically as such, and that therefore the community used its power to get the land as a "park," and proceeded immediately to make the land an airport without any great attention to the logic of this proceeding, but only to its immediate effectiveness.

[1] See Appendix 23, Airports Built on Park Lands.

RELATION TO THE PUBLIC UTILITY SYSTEM

The airport must have adequate fire protection, adequate water supply for other purposes, an adequate sewerage system which is not likely to be very great, a sufficient gas system in many cases, and certainly ample electric power and light supply. The effect of these requirements on the choice of a location of the airport is obvious. There is one particular, however, already referred to, which might even be a governing factor in the choice of an airport location. This is that the surface drainage from an airport need not be particularly unsanitary, and the amount of sewage from an airport is so small as to be capable of local treatment without necessarily calling for any discharge into a general sewerage system. This means that in an airport a city has a necessary and large area which might be located in places which were perfectly suitable for an airport but which, if developed for residence or any other use which caused considerable density of occupancy, would cost for sewerage an amount out of all reasonable proportion with the resultant taxable value of the land.

ZONING FOR AIRPORTS [1]

It would seem to be impossible to create a special zone for each airport. It is true that we have in the past in some instances done "spot zoning" which created smaller zones than the area of one airport. But to incorporate the airport locations in the zoning plan, thereby fixing them with the degree of definiteness and permanence which such a plan entails, would be to make definite a provision for the future which cannot now be accurately predicted, and perhaps to commit the city to an expenditure of money for such future provision out of all proportion with present financial possibility. Moreover, the airport is primarily a part of a transportation system, and the application of zoning to a transportation system is full of difficulties. Privately owned and operated airports are legal and presumably desirable, and the application of zoning to such ports, making each separate private venture a zone in itself, would again be full of great difficulties, both legal and administrative.

Ordinarily the airport would be located in an outlying residential district because this district has the greatest area, the least intensive development, and the fewest streets, but the airport might in a special case be located in any one of the zoned districts. As its location is of

[1] See also pp. 121–22 and 126–28 for further discussion of Zoning for Airports.

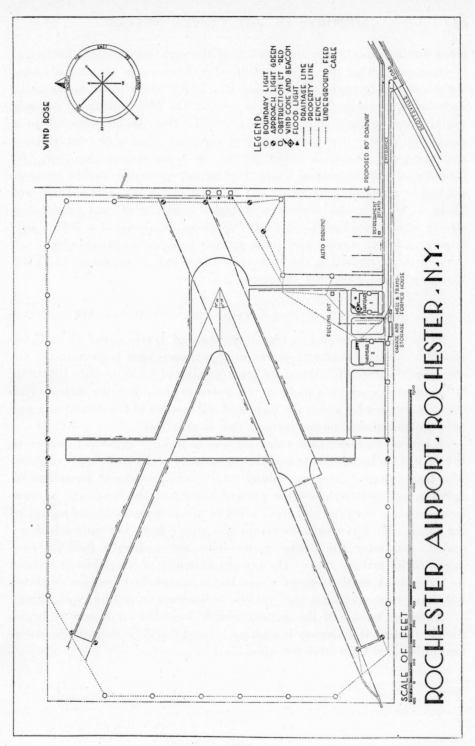

ROCHESTER AIRPORT· ROCHESTER· N·Y·

WIND ROSE

LEGEND
BOUNDARY LIGHT
APPROACH LIGHT GREEN
OBSTRUCTION L'T 'RED
WIND CONE AND BEACON
FLOOD LIGHT
DRAINAGE LINE
PROPERTY LINE
FENCE
UNDERGROUND FEED
CABLE

SCALE OF FEET

AUTO PARKING

FUELING PIT

HANGAR 1

HANGAR 2

GARAGE AND
STORAGE

WELL & TRANS-
FORMER HOUSE

ENTRANCE

PROPOSED 80' ROADWAY

SCOTTSVILLE ROAD

DECENBERMENT
STAND

great public importance, and worthy of the greatest care and publicity, it would seem that the best procedure, in fairness to all interests concerned, should be to consider the airport as a use which would be normally excluded from residential districts, *except* that the Zoning Board of Appeals would have the right and duty to grant locations for airports within a residential zone on the presentation of sufficient proof of the convenience and necessity of such a public service in some specific location. In commercial and industrial zones, the airport probably should be considered as admissible by right, but in these zones, of course, there are likely to be high land values and many constructed and established streets which would make it both expensive to assemble a sufficiently large area for an airport and unlikely that so large an area could be set aside without upsetting the city plan to an extent to which the City Planning Board ought not to accede.

Appearance of the City as Seen from the Air

Even now, although in a transitory state of development, the airport should be at least neat and decent in appearance, seen both from the air and from the ground. When we know enough of its immediate future to be justified in making a more or less permanent design, the airport, like every other area by which the taste and self-respect of the community are to be judged, should be beautiful as well as practical.

A general consideration which we believe to be of great importance is the duty of the municipality and the region not to offer to the sight of those who travel over it by air anything unnecessarily offensive by reason of ugliness, and not to deface the present beauty of the landscape as seen from above. The principal application of this is in the matter of advertising signs. We have seen the landscape visible from our railroads desecrated, and later the public views from our highways polluted and exploited for private gain. The present difficulty of the public in getting its rights back in these cases is due to the intrenched position of those who have been making a very profitable business from this exploitation.

A similar misuse of the scenery visible from the air is sure to begin soon, — indeed it is already beginning, — and it will be much more easily forestalled now than later remedied.

CHAPTER III

RELATION OF THE AIRPORT
TO THE NATIONAL TRANSPORTATION NET

AIRWAYS

SO far we have been discussing local and municipal considerations. There are also important and perhaps decisive influences affecting the airport which are of a regional and perhaps national character, and have to do with the relation of the airport to the great national net of routes of travel, both through the air and by railway.

Early in the study of the airport site, it should be determined whether the city is on a regional or national airway route, existing or planned, or reasonably to be predicted. If the city is not and is not likely to be on such a route, then it should be considered whether or not the distance from the city to the nearest airport which is on such a route is so great that people can save enough time by flying, as compared with other means of transportation, to warrant a local airport for this purpose. It is evident that any time up to perhaps half an hour might be consumed by a person in town in getting from his residence or from his place of business to the airport. If now it takes him only fifteen minutes to fly from the local airport to an airport on the main airway, it might actually save him time to make the whole of this journey by automobile or possibly by railroad, in which case the local airport would serve only local needs and not be particularly valuable as a connection with the general national airway net.

If the town is on a main airway route, then the function of this route in the entire airway system should be considered as a means of predicting the amount and kind of future travel by air over it, and consequently the size and kind of the airport. It would make a great difference in the choice of a site whether the air route was to be used by landplanes or by seaplanes or by both; and it should be considered whether the traffic was passenger traffic or express traffic or mail delivery, or, — if it consisted of all three of these, as it probably would, — what were their relative proportions.

37

Any decisions as to the airport will further be influenced by what kind of station on this route the local airport is going to be. To borrow the language of the railroad, will the local airport be a terminal, a junction point, a regular stop, a flag stop, or, although it is along the route, will it be so located that no stop could profitably be made by long-distance traffic except under extraordinary circumstances? If it is a terminal station, then terminal storage facilities will be necessary, and a close coördination must be arranged between the long-distance traffic by air and local air traffic, or other forms of transportation, presumably radiating from the terminal airport and serving a local region. If it be a junction point, an intersection of two airways, then transfer facilities will need to be given special consideration. If it be a regular stop for practically all service, then the capacity of the airport must keep pace with the whole capacity of the airway as it grows. If, however, the airport is what might be called a flag stop, the field must still be large enough to accommodate any transportation units which are used on the route, but the intensity of use of the field will be much less than the intensity of use of the airway.

It might happen that the proposed local field would lie on the line of a main airway, but since it lay between two large cities which were not very far apart as air transport takes account of distance, there would be no advantage to through traffic in making a stop at this local port. This would mean, of course, that the field could, and probably would, serve the purpose of an intermediate and emergency landing field, but that otherwise the air traffic related to it would be as local as though the field were not on a main air route at all.

RAILWAYS

If the city is on a railroad trunk line, is it so located that it is a logical transfer point from railway to air and vice versa on a transcontinental combined air-rail journey? This point is not easily determined, because it will vary with the railway schedules. At present it is not uncommon to travel by train at night and travel by airplane by day, and the transfer points would thus be at the places where the most popular trains found themselves at the end of the day or night. It should be borne in mind also that we do not know how long this form of transfer from railway to air will remain effective and popular.

Another consideration, if the town is on a railroad trunk line, is the size of the surrounding region tributary to the city, either by train or by air; that is, from what cities round about, not on the main line, might planes come in order to make railroad connections, or might people come by railway in order to make air connections?

If the city is on a railroad spur line, or not on a railroad line at all, the same question which arose in discussing the requirements of the airport not on an airway route arises in a slightly different form. For those who wish to take a train on the main line, would enough time be saved by flying to an airport on the main line, over the time which would be spent by getting to the same point by railway, by automobile, or by other means of transportation, to justify the construction of an airport as a means of regional communication? If an existing spur line or a spur line which might profitably be built would save more time than an airport would in this regard, then again the airport is only of local efficiency.

HIGHWAYS

The same general considerations apply to the relation of the airport to the national highway net that have already been discussed in regard to its relation to the national railway net, except, of course, that transportation by road is not quite so certain as by railway, — particularly in bad weather, — it is not so cheap, and for any considerable distances it is not so fast. On the other hand the private automobile traveling by road wastes less of the passenger's time in getting started than does either the railroad train or the airplane, and so is not competed with by either until distance overcomes this initial advantage.

WATERWAYS

If the transportation by a main waterway with which connection is to be made by airplane is by means of ships, and the waterway touches the town where the airport is to be located, obviously there is a great advantage from this point of view in locating the airport where it will serve as a means of transfer from air transportation to water transportation, without intermediate loss of time. This would be equally true if the transportation over the water were by dirigibles, which are likely to be used over long-distance water routes, rather than over land routes, on account of their having a greater ability than have airplanes to remain in the air under all circumstances. The same advantage of being a point of transfer, however, would apply if the water route were used for shorter along-shore flights by seaplanes, to which form of conveyance people might change from landplanes at the port.

Some airports will be ports of entry from other countries, with the requirement of special facilities for this use. Much more might be said of such special cases, but we do not attempt in this discussion, or indeed elsewhere in the report, to cover all the possibilities which might logically be expected, but only those which experience has already shown are to be important in the air navigation of the future.

AIRPORT ADMINISTRATION

By

MILLER McCLINTOCK

Lecturer and Director of the Bureau for Municipal Research and Director of the
Albert Russel Erskine Bureau for Street Traffic Research, Harvard University

and

PAUL MAHONEY

Now Assistant in the Transportation and Communication Department of the
Chamber of Commerce of the United States of America

INTRODUCTION

The enthusiasm for aviation which has swept the country during the past decade, and especially during the past three years, has resulted in certain tendencies with respect to public ownership and management which may or may not be sound. This report is in no manner designed to afford a definite or final answer to the many problems which these tendencies have raised. Rather it is an attempt to relate what has been done under typical circumstances, and to emphasize the factors which must be considered in evaluating the present status and future development of airport ownership and management.

It is significant that a majority of the important air terminals now in use are under public ownership and management. This situation has without question resulted from a widespread feeling that the infant industry of air transport, and aviation in general, is of such a character as to warrant a public subsidy.

How long will this necessity last, if indeed it exists, and where will it eventually lead? Perhaps the time has come to ask whether the future of aviation will be most securely fostered by a public ownership of terminal facilities. The answer may be in the affirmative, but if so, it must be justified as a definite departure from American practice with respect to transportation terminals in general.

A similar but no less important question relates to the actual management and operation of airports. Are cities capable of successfully undertaking the detailed operation of air terminals, with their many technical and experimental problems? Again the answer may be in the affirmative, but it is apparent that assurance of success will depend largely upon the capacity of cities to develop administrative organizations and fiscal policies suited to the unusual requirements of airport management and operation.

As has been stated above, it is not the purpose of this report to answer these questions in a definitive manner. The development of airports has been so recent and is still of such an experimental character that a final answer would be impossible. The answer, however, must be honestly sought, and each new development must be submitted to the critical test of its logical relation to the economic and political structure of the community rather than judged by its mere coincidence with popular enthusiasm.

These logical tests are neither new nor mysterious.   They have long been a part of the policy of municipal management in American cities. It is hoped that the materials presented in this report may be of assistance to citizens and public officials in guiding the aviation activities of their communities, in order that each community may obtain its fair share of the benefits of air travel, and especially that the business of aviation may develop upon the most stable of foundations.

CHAPTER I

OWNERSHIP

AIRPORTS have existed since the first successful flight was made, for the airport is as necessary to the plane as the road is to the automobile. It was some time, however, before the airport acquired definite characteristics.

Until the war the airplane was such an outstanding novelty that its exhibition in flight was its first civil function. Airports were usually simple, temporary fields adequate for the demands of the few civil planes in operation. The problem of providing facilities for the increased number of planes during the war was met by the military and naval branches of the government.

When the armistice released thousands of trained pilots and large numbers of surplus planes, the business of making the American public air-minded was begun. Need for more adequate civil airports was foreseen and some development undertaken. Unfortunately, the unstable and relatively unremunerative nature of commercial aviation just after the war did not attract sufficient capital to provide adequate facilities.

The Kelly Air Mail Act of 1925 was a stimulus for a new phase of operation: the established long-distance air route, flown on schedule with mail, passengers, and express.[1]

By the end of 1926 the war surplus of aircraft had become exhausted, and new construction began in earnest. The Air Commerce Act of that year provided the necessary governmental machinery to encourage and regulate the use of aircraft in commerce.

In 1927 aviation was popularized by the feats of such intrepid aviators as Lindbergh, Chamberlin, Maitland, Hegenberger, Byrd, Balchen, Bronte, Goebel, Schulter, Brock, Schlee, and Haldeman. Air transportation had become a fact. But what of the airports?

---

[1] For further description of this period of development, see "Civil Aeronautics in the United States," U. S. Dept. of Commerce, Aeronautics Branch, Aeronautics Bulletin No. 1, Mar. 15, 1928.

Ownership of Airports

With the increased production and operation of planes, with popular interest assured, and with a realization that the lack of landing facilities was in great measure retarding the development of aviation, municipalities, advised and encouraged by the Department of Commerce, enthusiastically undertook the task of providing airports.

Records of the Department of Commerce show that at the end of 1927 there were 240 municipal airports and 263 private and commercial airports. At the end of 1928 there were 368 municipal airports and 365 private and commercial airports. Figures for 1929 show 453 municipal airports and 495 private and commercial airports.[1]

Of the airports studied, there were established:

Before 1920 . . . . %

During 1920 . . . . 4%	During 1925 . . . . 7%
" 1921 . . . . 3%	" 1926 . . . . 18%
" 1922 . . . . 0%	" 1927 . . . . 16%
" 1923 . . . . 0%	" 1928 . . . . 23%
" 1924 . . . . 2%	" 1929 . . . . 20%

At the time of their establishment 59 per cent were private and 41 per cent were public ventures, while 34 per cent of these private ventures have since been taken over by municipalities.

These figures do not cover all the airports throughout the country. Nevertheless, it is believed that they furnish a fair index of the trend in ownership and development of the more important airports.

The question of public or private ownership of airports will probably exert in the future, as it has in the past, a basic influence on the development of air transportation. The number of airports already in existence represents a capital outlay of many millions of dollars, and constitutes a utility of great importance.

So accessible have city treasuries been to the demands for public funds for airport construction, and so convinced are public and private agencies generally that airport ownership is a normal and proper public function, that any question of its propriety may appear irrelevant. If its basis is sound, no harm can result. However, if there are legitimate questions which can be raised, it is assuredly time that correct answers be sought.

[1] "Air Commerce Bulletin," Vol. I, No. 17, p. 9. U. S. Dept. of Commerce, Aeronautics Branch. Mar. 1, 1930.

Courtesy of Fairfax Airports, Inc.

TERMINAL BUILDING, FAIRFAX AIRPORT, KANSAS CITY, KANSAS

It is possible that by an analysis of the functions performed by the airport, and by analogy with other transportation facilities, guiding principles can be established. The functions of the general airport are diversified. It is a place of arrival and departure for passengers, mail, express, and freight. In addition it must provide storage and service facilities for the transportation units. It may be called upon to serve as a base for training students, and for the testing of planes. Many ports also serve as quasi-recreational centers for those engaged in sport flying. These functions represent elements of both public and private interest.

OWNERSHIP OF TERMINAL FACILITIES IN OTHER FORMS OF TRANSPORTATION

The airport has no exact analogy in other forms of transportation. There are, however, many significant similarities.

RAIL TRANSPORTATION

Rail terminals for passengers, mail, express, and freight, and terminals for servicing of equipment and storage of material, are exclusively under private ownership. This follows naturally from the close functional and physical relation which such terminals have to the privately owned railroads.

The public interest in rail common carriers is strong. In the provision of adequate terminal facilities and in their management this interest has been protected through the medium of state and federal control; but even in the construction and maintenance of union terminal facilities there has been little public participation. The principle which has apparently guided railway terminal development has been that the railroad being privately owned, the terminal should likewise be privately owned, but adequately controlled to protect the public.

In the early days of railway development state and local governments extended various types of subsidies to encourage railway expansion, but these subsidies never took the form of providing privately owned transportation companies with publicly owned and maintained terminal facilities.

WATER TRANSPORTATION

Practice with respect to water terminals is not so uniform as in the case of rail terminals. That part of the port composed of navigable waters is uniformly under public ownership and public control. Major improvements such as channels and breakwaters are dredged or built with public funds. Marginal lands are frequently owned by the state or local political jurisdiction.

The terminal facilities themselves, consisting of docks, warehouses, and other equipment, may be either publicly or privately owned. Public ownership of dock facilities where followed has been justified partially as a subsidy to stimulate port activity.

AUTOMOTIVE TRANSPORTATION

Airports have frequently been compared to the highway or street system. The analogy is exact only in so far as it may be said that both are essential for their respective forms of transportation. The functions are quite different. The principal similarity between the airport and the street system occurs when the latter is used for parking purposes, either for the temporary storage of the vehicle, or for the transfer of passengers or merchandise. By analogy streets are more similar to improved airways than to airports.

The airport itself is comparable to parking and garage facilities. There are few examples of publicly owned garages or parking spaces, private ownership being the rule.

CONCLUSIONS WITH RESPECT TO ANALOGOUS TYPES OF TERMINAL FACILITIES

A review of these analogies indicates a definite tendency toward private ownership. There seems to be nothing in the functional characteristics of airports to differentiate them materially from those of other forms of transportation. This conclusion does not necessarily indicate that public ownership of airports is undesirable, but it does indicate that where followed it is a departure from general American practice.

Is the Public Ownership of Airports Good Practice?

There are many opponents of the public ownership of any utility who consequently oppose the public ownership of airports. Despite the arguments they advance in opposition to such ownership, numerous municipal airports and some state and county airports exist. The legal validity of public airport ownership has been established on several occasions.[1]

Even though the municipal ownership of airports may be considered a legal and possibly desirable governmental function, there still remains

[1] See p. 117, for discussion of the establishment of an airport as a "Public Purpose."

a practical problem. Will the community and aviation best be served by such ownership? [1] The proper test of the validity of these theories of ownership is the manner in which they have demonstrated their efficacy in practice.

IMMEDIATE FACILITIES MADE POSSIBLE

Observation indicates that municipal ownership of airports has accomplished certain definite things. Private investment in airports is limited to areas of possible immediate profit. This is not true of public funds; consequently, through municipal ownership the community has been able to enjoy the facilities of an airport sooner than would have been possible otherwise. While the commercial airport management may have an excellent program of improvement, it must proceed gradually, relating its investment to anticipated revenue. Municipal airports, on the contrary, can be provided with adequate equipment far more rapidly. It is not surprising to find that a majority of the more important airports in the United States have been developed under public ownership.

INTANGIBLE BENEFITS PROTECTED

The effect of municipal ownership of the airport on the citizen is similar to the municipal ownership of any public utility. Under either type of ownership, the public bears the cost of the direct benefits when it avails itself of the convenience of air transportation. Under municipal ownership the public must also pay, in effect, for the intangible benefits. Placing the city on the air map and the consequent possible increase in the city's business activity, or the savings made possible by air transport, are of general potential benefit. The guarantee of future air transportation is of considerable importance.

The ultimate value of these intangible benefits cannot be calculated in a period of development. At present it can only be said that the municipalities, in general, provide a larger and better equipped airport than private interests are likely to furnish, and the public must pay in proportion though the majority make no direct use of the facilities provided.

COÖRDINATION AND MANAGEMENT

The opportunities of coördinating the port facilities with the city plan and of obtaining public service facilities such as water, sewerage,

[1] See Appendix 24, Opinions on the Public Ownership of Airports.

storm drains, and highway connections are increased under municipal ownership. Municipal airports in general, however, are no better located than those commercially operated. In fact, the commercial venture has one distinct advantage, for its choice of site is not limited by political boundaries.[1]

Management of the municipal airport is not superior to management of the commercial airport. For economic reasons a higher degree of efficiency is demanded of the management of the latter, though it is not always demonstrated in practice.

EFFECT UPON AVIATION

Aviation has indisputably been benefited by the municipal airport. The number of adequate airports has been tremendously increased. Municipal ownership has given an air of permanence to aviation ventures which has encouraged commercial investment. Charges for services rendered and facilities provided have been based on the operator's ability to pay rather than on the basis of cost plus interest on investment. Consequently aviation has been indirectly subsidized by the public, and the growth of aviation artificially stimulated. It is for the future to decide whether forced growth with its attendant danger of temporary overdevelopment is more costly than the delay entailed by slower and more cautious growth.

The United States has long since gone on record as believing in the merits of subsidizing infant industry by protection. The granting of subsidy through the provision of terminal facilities is nevertheless a practice which has few parallels. Public ownership of river and harbor terminal facilities is perhaps the only outstanding comparable development.

OWNERSHIP MUST ULTIMATELY BE BASED ON SOUND ECONOMICS

Problems of development are but temporary, however. The coördination of the airport with the city plan is of primary importance. Ultimate objectives include the provision of adequate transportation facilities, and the satisfactory operation of the airport from the standpoint of both cost and service rendered.

It is believed that these objectives can be attained eventually without public ownership. With air transportation well established, it is

[1] The Central Airport at Camden, N. J., serves Philadelphia, Pa. The Curtiss-Steinberg Airport in East St. Louis, Ill., serves St. Louis, Mo. The latter port is far more conveniently located than the St. Louis Municipal Airport, St. Louis, Mo.

reasonable to assume that if an airport cannot be made to pay there is no need for it. Regulation of its location and operation are matters of planning and legislation. It has not been demonstrated that better results in regard to these features are assured under municipal ownership.

It has been the experience of this country that, where private ownership of commercial activities which are colored with public interest can be regulated for general benefit, it offers a satisfactory method. When aviation has reached its commercial majority, there should be little need for the municipal ownership of airports. In the meantime the development of airports must parallel and even anticipate the growth of aviation. Ownership of the airport is influenced by current needs, but in the determination of the ownership of any contemplated airport these needs should be closely analyzed.

Predominant Use as a Factor in Airport Ownership [1]

Predominant use is of primary importance in determining the type of ownership. It has been assumed that with the development of aviation certain types of airports will come into existence as a result of segregation of use.

TYPES OF USE BEST ADAPTED TO PRIVATE OWNERSHIP

Club, factory, school, and transport base airports are exclusive in their nature and are purely private in their purpose. There is a strong presumption against public ownership. However, these functional uses may be properly a minor and incidental part of the activities of a public port, as long as they do not interfere with its proper operation.

USE WHICH INVOLVES PUBLIC INTEREST

There are certain other types of ports, the use of which is more general and more public in character, for which the question of ownership cannot be decided so definitely. There are many authorities who foresee and advocate the "downtown" airport, located as close to the heart of the city as possible, and highly specialized in use. This port will serve as a central station for the transfer of passengers, mail, and express. The planes using it will be stored and repaired elsewhere. Whether it be on the waterfront, over freight yards, on the top of a large building or buildings, or in some conveniently located open space, the great cost and the difficulty of obtaining land will limit its size. Moreover, the tremen-

[1] See pp. 20–24, for functional classification of airports.

dous volume of air traffic which would justify its existence would restrict its use in order to insure the maximum efficiency of operation. There would be probably not more than one airport of this type in any large city. Therefore the problem of location and of restriction, and the necessity of granting equal privileges to legitimate users, would require a high degree of public control. It is apparent that the public interest would be substantial, and unless regulation of private ownership proved adequate, public ownership might be indicated, as has often been the case in harbor facilities, though rarely with rail terminals.

The ports located in the suburbs, serving outlying communities, and the airports located near rapid transit lines just outside the more densely settled portion of the city, would be much more general in their use, and their functions would vary with the demands of the areas which they served. The operation of these airports will undoubtedly call for a large amount of public control, and in some cases may justify public ownership and management.

At present most communities are served by one airport which performs a combination of services. It is usually a passenger, mail, express, and freight depot, a service, storage, school, and factory base. Serving as it does both public and private interests, a determination of its proper ownership must depend on other factors than use, unless it is apparent that some particular use will rapidly become dominant.

State and County Airport Ownership

There are few examples of state or county airport ownership. Ten county airports [1] are listed by the Department of Commerce. Rhode Island has created a state airport commission with powers to acquire land for a state airport. [2]

Many municipal airports, however, are located outside of the municipal boundaries. [3] In some cases this has presented certain difficulties. A problem encountered when the municipal airport is located in adjacent

---

[1] Kern County Airport, Calif.; Imperial County Airport, Calif.; Menominee County Airport, Mich.; Muskegon County Airport, Mich.; Burlington County Aero Club Field, N. J.; Josephine County Airport, Ore.; Franklin County Airport, Wash.; Yakima County Airport, Wash.; Jackson County Airport, Wis.; Milwaukee County Airport, Wis. From "Airports and Landing Fields," U. S. Dept. of Commerce, Aeronautics Branch, Aeronautics Bulletin No. 5, Revised Jan. 1, 1930. Wayne County Airport, Mich., which was visited during the field survey is not listed. There are, perhaps, other county airports nearing completion which have been omitted.

[2] "State Aeronautical Legislation and Compilation of State Laws," U. S. Dept. of Commerce, Aeronautics Branch, Aeronautics Bulletin No. 18.

[3] See Appendix 25, Municipalities where Airports are Outside the Corporate Limits.

DETROIT CITY AIRPORT — AN INTOWN AIRPORT

non-municipal territory is that of taxation. Another is that of land condemnation, which in some cases has hindered the acquisition of land for the airport as well as right of way for direct highway routes.

State legislation has been resorted to for the solution of certain of these problems. Joint responsibilities and joint interest in the airport have been recognized, as in the formation in Louisville of an airport board on which both the city and county are represented.[1]

DUPLICATION OF AIRPORT FACILITIES

At least two counties have established airports not far from municipal airports serving the same communities. These are Wayne County Airport, near Detroit, and Milwaukee County Airport, near Milwaukee. It is possible that the demands of aviation will increase to such an extent in the future that such duplication of terminal facilities will not prove wasteful. Nevertheless, airport costs are so large, the possibilities of immediate profit from their operation so small, and the experience in airport management so limited, that close coöperation between the city and the county is obviously highly desirable.

CONCLUSION

It is apparent that the municipal airport has played an important part in the development of air transportation in the United States by supplying an indirect subsidy in the form of essential terminal facilities. Such a subsidy may be justified by the special character and present status of air transport, but cities should not lose sight of the fact that it is a departure from generally established practice. Evidence indicates that while the need for this type of subsidy is rapidly on the wane, there are other factors which will continue to promote the development of municipal airports. It is also apparent that the creation of municipal airports to meet present needs establishes municipal airport ownership on a basis which is likely to have little relation to future problems. The conclusion may thus be drawn that municipalities should limit their participation in aviation to creation of those airports in which there is a predominant public interest, and only in such cases where there exists no possibility of supplying adequate terminal facilities by the encouragement and control of private enterprise.

[1] For organization of the Louisville and Jefferson County Air Board, see p. 61.

CHAPTER II

ADMINISTRATION

A IRPORT administration, like airport ownership, is a new departure in municipal government. Municipalities suddenly have found themselves confronted by new responsibilities without even the guidance of sound principles established by similar private ventures. Although the commercial air terminal demands no radical departures from conventional business administration and management, the task of fitting an airport into the already elaborate administrative machinery of most American cities obviously raises many new problems.

What department of the city government should be charged with airport control? Should a department be created for this new form of municipal activity, or should the airport and its administration be absorbed by a department whose existing facilities might be readily expanded?

The 85 airports visited and studied during the course of the survey include 47 municipal air terminals,[1] constituting outstanding examples of their kind in the United States. Five general types of administrative organization were disclosed. The administration of thirty-two (68 per cent) of the forty-seven municipal airports was by a preëxisting department. Ten of these thirty-two (or 21 per cent of the forty-seven) were administered by the park department, ten (21 per cent) by the department of public works, four (9 per cent) by the department of public service, and eight (17 per cent) by other established departments of the city government.

While the creation of a separate department of aeronautics is not the general practice, yet the significant proportion of the air terminals so administered, coupled with the relative size and importance of these airports, warrants examination of this type of procedure.

[1] These include two county airports, — Wayne County, Mich., and Milwaukee County, Wis.

ADMINISTRATION BY A SEPARATE DEPARTMENT OF AERONAUTICS

Fifteen cities with municipal airports of more than average importance are administered by separate agencies which have assumed full charge of all aeronautical activity. Twelve of these are administered by a Department of Aeronautics, and three by a Council Committee.[1]

THE DIRECTOR OF AERONAUTICS

In six cities the Department of Aeronautics is headed by a Director of Aeronautics. In Dallas, Los Angeles, Miami, and Ponca City such directors have been appointed. In Ponca City, however, the airport is operated by a private company and the director is an honorary appointee, drawing no salary. Fort Worth and Pontiac have provided for the appointment of a director of aeronautics but as yet have made no appointment.

In Miami, Ponca City, Pontiac, and Fort Worth appointments are made by the city manager. Los Angeles selects its director of aeronautics from the three candidates receiving the highest grades in a civil service examination for the position. In Dallas the mayor appoints the director of aeronautics with approval of the commission.

A director of aeronautics is usually placed in full charge of all the city's aviation activities, including the construction, improvement, maintenance, and operation of municipal landplane and seaplane bases. In practice, however, the development of aeronautical activity has not passed the point where the director's duties include much more than management of a single airport. Thus with few exceptions his duties are largely those of an airport manager. In fact, no additional appointment of an airport manager has been made in those cities which have filled the post of director of aeronautics. This condition, however, may be but temporary, for the time is perhaps not far off when the increase in aviation activity may so occupy the director of aeronautics with matters of general aeronautical policy that he will no longer be able to assume direct management of the airport. At present the salary of a director of aeronautics ranges from $2000 to $5000 a year.

THE AIR BOARD

In Hartford, Louisville, Memphis, Salisbury (N. C.), Winston-Salem, and Terre Haute the Department of Aeronautics is headed by an Air

[1] See Appendix 26, Secs. A, B, and C, "Cities Where the Airport Is Separately Administered."

Board. In each case the members serve without salary, but with a nominal allowance for expenses.

The merits of a board or a commission as opposed to a single director have been discussed at length throughout the history of municipal administration. The single executive rather than the board has gained increasing favor during the last few years in those departments requiring skilled administration, quick action, and undivided responsibility. The board has been retained in the administration of certain specialized functions where representation rather than responsibility appears more necessary. In airport administration undivided responsibility is deemed more important than representation; consequently there exists a presumption in favor of a single responsible executive.

THE COUNCIL COMMITTEE

Atlanta, Macon, and San Francisco have placed their airports under the control of Council Committees. The Atlanta committee is composed of five members, and the Macon and San Francisco committees of three members. Despite the fact that many activities of municipal government are satisfactorily administered by council committees, airport control presents many problems of such a technical nature that it is questionable whether this type of administration will prove effective.

FACTORS GOVERNING THE CREATION OF A SEPARATE DEPARTMENT

The independent department affords a suitable administrative agency, but it may not be wise in all cases to add to the already complex structure of the city government. What factors should be considered before creating such a department?

Some cities have sufficient power under the terms of their charter to create additional departments of the city government. In a great many cities, however, an act of the state legislature is necessary before an additional department can be created.[1]

Granting that the city has the power to create a separate department of aeronautics, the additional expense involved by the creation of such a department is another factor to be considered. The advantages of a separate department for airport matters should be carefully weighed with the expense involved in comparison to the expense and possible advantages of consolidation with some existing department.

[1] See pp. 118–19, for discussion of the power of the local government to establish an airport.

Courtesy of Board of Port Commissioners, Port of Oakland, Calif.

OAKLAND AIRPORT

Present conditions should not be the only factor influencing the creation of a separate department. Possibilities of future aeronautical development should be considered in the light of the city's relation to the airways network, its topographical situation, and its industrial position.

Finally the size of the city and its form of government may exert a determining influence on the question. The fifteen cities in which the airports are independently administered vary in size from Los Angeles to Ponca City.[1] Of these the three cities which placed their airports under a council committee had, of course, a mayor-council form of government. Of the remaining twelve which had created a separate department, five were governed by a mayor and council, two by a commission, and five by a city manager.

The Airport under a Preëxisting Department

It is significant that out of forty-seven municipal airports, twenty were found to be under the control of the department of public works[2] and the park department,[3] and twelve under some other already established department of government.[4] The preponderance of favor lies with the department of public works and the park department. There are sharp differences of opinion, however, over which of these two departments is the better fitted for airport administration.

THE AIRPORT UNDER THE PARK DEPARTMENT

It is said that the Park Department should administer the airport because the requirements are similar to those met in park development and administration. Thus for both airports and parks a large tract of land must be cleared, graded, drained, surfaced, and landscaped. Structures must be erected and concessions leased or operated, and provision must be made for the handling of large crowds. It is reasoned that because of these similarities the park department possesses valuable experience which should be utilized in airport administration, and that savings will result from a more efficient use of materials and personnel.

[1] See Appendix 2, Population of Cities Visited.
[2] See Appendix 27, Cities where the Department of Public Works is in Charge of the Airport.
[3] See Appendix 28, Cities where the Department of Parks is in Charge of the Airport.
[4] See Appendix 29, Cities where the Department of Public Service is in Charge of the Airport, and Appendix 30, Cities and Counties where the Airport is Administered by Other Departments.

THE AIRPORT UNDER THE DEPARTMENT OF PUBLIC WORKS

Advocates of airport administration by the Department of Public Works advance similar arguments. The department of public works has also the necessary experience, equipment, and personnel to construct and maintain an airport. Close coöperation with the engineering staff is assured, for the type of work is similar to that which constantly engages the attention of the department. It is unnecessary to present this argument in more detail, so exactly does it parallel that advanced by the advocates of park administration.

Some doubt as to the value of these arguments is suggested by one writer who says: "One might just as logically combine the airport with the school system." [1] Both demand land acquisition, building construction and administration, open area maintenance, swimming pool and tennis court management, restauranting, and good public relations policy.

The ultimate decision whether the airport should be placed under the park or public works department will be determined in a great measure by local conditions. The ports which are now found under one of these two departments are there, in most cases, because of chance rather than careful consideration of the relative merits of each. The reasons advanced in field interviews include: "it was politically advisable"; "the commissioner was an aviation enthusiast"; "no other place to put it"; "the park department was the only one that could acquire the land, so called it an air park"; "everything new is put in the department of public works"; "office of manager was abolished, manager became director of public works, took the airport with him"; "park commissioners were interested."

However, it is indisputable that the primary function of aviation is transportation. This being so, the administration of the airport is a technical function, the successful performance of which is of importance to the entire city. The department of public works is likely to have wider engineering experience than the park department. The former is concerned daily with the combined interests of the city, while the park department deals with but one special phase of municipal activity, — recreation. It would appear, therefore, that if the airport is to be placed in an existing department, it logically belongs in the department of public works rather than in any other, subject of course to special local conditions.

[1] "Airport Management an Independent Function," by Ernest P. Goodrich. *City Planning* April, 1930, p. 122.

Two cities have placed the airport under the Harbor Board or Board of Port Commissioners. This course may be logical when the airport is located on property belonging to the board. Oakland has successfully correlated the activities of the port and the airport and has placed the care of their development under one head. In the other instance, a good county airport is serving the community. The municipal airport is so badly located as to make expenditures for improvement sheer waste. In consequence it is given little attention by the municipal harbor board.

THE QUASI-PUBLIC CORPORATION

The plan of putting the administration and operation of a combination of rail, water, and air terminals under a quasi-public corporation has been suggested and widely discussed. Such a plan has been advocated for Philadelphia.[1] The plan suggests a corporation

to be known as The Philadelphia Terminal, of which the City of Philadelphia will be the owner, this corporation to have a Board of Directors, which will be automatically appointed by reason of positions which they hold.

The following officials or their nominees are suggested:

The Mayor of the City of Philadelphia
The President of the City Council
Director of the Wharton School, University of Pennsylvania
Chairman of the Public Service Commission of the Commonwealth
     of Pennsylvania
President of the Chamber of Commerce
President of the Board of Trade
President of the Maritime Exchange
Governor of the Federal Reserve Bank
President of the Engineers Club
Head of the Department of Economics and Transportation at
     Temple University
President of the Pennsylvania Railroad
Chairman of the Philadelphia Business Progress Committee
Director of Wharves, Docks, and Ferries
President of the Philadelphia and Reading Railway Co.
Chairman, State Aeronautics Commission
Presiding Officer, Local Chapter, National Aeronautic Association
The Manager or Representative of the lessee of the airport

[1] "A Plan for the Development of the Philadelphia Terminal Air-Marine-Rail." The Philadelphia Business Progress Committee, Sept. 6, 1929.

The entire terminal will then be leased by the city to this corporation at a rental which will be 100% of the net income. The Board of Directors will elect the officers of the Company and appoint those to be responsible for its development and administration, to serve with or without pay. . . .

It will be the duty of the directors to recommend to the city the development which the city itself should undertake, or to sublet to private interests on appropriate terms, certain portions of the tract.

This combination of terminals would not always be possible, but the plan might be used for the single purpose of airport development and administration. It is apparent, however, that the necessity for such an elaborate organization is less when a consolidation of several terminal facilities is not contemplated.

The Advisory Board

The Advisory Board is common in airport administration. Thirteen of the municipalities studied have made provision for such a board.[1] In many others, though no such provision has been made, a similar influence is exercised either by the aviation committee of the Chamber of Commerce, the aviation committee of the local post of the American Legion, or by a local Aero Club.

The smallest board among those observed by us is composed of three members, the largest of twenty-four, the usual number being five or seven. Among the interests represented on the various boards are the executive branch of the municipal government, represented by the mayor; the legislative branch, by aldermen and councilmen; the airport itself, by the director in whose charge it had been placed; education, by members of the school board and, less frequently, the president of the local university; aviation interests, by those engaged in this business; and the public, by outstanding business and professional men of the city.

The qualifications required of appointees are interest in aviation and some official connection with the body they represent. In most cases the members are appointed by the mayor or manager with or without the approval of the council or commission; in a few cases they are appointed by the head of the department operating the airport. The term of office of the members runs from one to six years with a usual term of three years.

Legally the powers of such boards are purely advisory. Actually

[1] See Appendix 31, Cities which Provide Airport Advisory Boards.

they all have gone through or are going through a process of evolution. In almost every case the original members of these boards were among those who made the airport possible. Usually these are farsighted, capable men, engaged in private business, interested in their city, and enthusiastic about aviation. Consequently, these boards are able to wield an influence far exceeding their legal powers. This influence is obviously an aid to prompt development and completion of the airport.

With the airport once established, however, it has been observed that the interest of the original members is inclined to wane. Eventually they tend in practice to become purely advisory, exerting but little of their former influence. The advisory board may be a highly desirable aid in the administration of the airport. It provides representation for a wide diversity of interests; its powers are limited only by its ability; it so functions that it almost always is likely to do more good than harm; and when the period of its usefulness is over, its activities may be assumed by a more formal organization.

THE PLACE OF THE AIRPORT IN THE COUNTY

Cases of county ownership and operation of the airport are few as compared to the number of airports municipally owned and operated. As already stated [1] there are only ten listed as county airports by the Department of Commerce: two in California, two in Michigan, one in New Jersey, one in Oregon, two in Washington, and two in Wisconsin. The tendency in county administration is to put the airport under the highway or park commission, instead of creating a special commission. As to the relative merits of county highway and park administration, the same factors apply as in the case of municipal departments of public works and parks.

An interesting attempt at joint control has been made in Louisville with the creation of the Louisville and Jefferson County Air Board. It is composed of six members appointed by the mayor and the county judge, all appointments terminating simultaneously at four-year periods. Equal representation of the Republican and Democratic parties is required. Members draw no salary, and are in complete charge of the airport, acting through the airport manager. This is a farsighted recognition of the fact that the problems of the airport or airport system are of more than local interest, and in many cases are of as much interest to the county as to the city.

[1] For the names of these airports, see p. 52, footnote 1.

Conclusion

A uniform type of airport administration can hardly be expected, nor would it be altogether wise. However, the development of airports has reached that point where cities are becoming increasingly interested in and guided by the methods and experience of other cities. Consequently it is reasonable to expect that airport administration will be limited to several distinctive types. An increase in the number of separate departments of aeronautics can be expected with an increase in aviation activity, and a wider recognition of local requirements by state legislatures.

Thus far it is significant that airport administration is affected favorably or adversely not by the form of administration but by the caliber of the department head and the political standards of the municipality.

CHAPTER III

MANAGEMENT

CITIES which have embarked on the business of furnishing terminal facilities for air transportation are faced with two alternatives in the actual management of these facilities. They may develop the organization and personnel with which to assume active and direct management of the airport, or they may relieve themselves of these responsibilities by leasing the airport for operation by private interests, retaining only general supervisory control in such broad matters of policy as may be incorporated in the terms of the lease.

Leasing the Municipal Airport

It is logical to inquire whether airport management, as distinguished from ownership, is a proper function of municipal activity. All evidence points to the fact that it is so considered, though in many respects it may be a distinct departure from conventional practice.

A factor in determining the choice between leasing and direct operation is the city's legal and financial status. Are there legal restrictions on the city's ability to engage in this type of enterprise? If so, what enabling legislation will be required to eliminate the obstacles, and how difficult will the enactment of this legislation prove to be?

The cost of operating and maintaining an airport equipped with adequate and modern facilities involves large expenditures which may not always be compensated by operating revenues. Is the city in a financial position to make these expenditures and to continue to maintain the airport in a satisfactory condition? How will potential operating revenue compare with the revenue to be derived from leasing, provided responsible and capable private interests can be found?

Also consideration should be given as to whether leasing the airport will be in harmony with the circumstances which originally dictated municipal ownership. If a desire to aid and encourage local aviation progress was the primary factor in the creation of the municipal airports,

63

will private operation, with its attendant need for larger and more immediate profit, stand as an obstacle in the path of such progress?[1]

As aviation grows and prospers, this question will become less important. Proper control of the airport, on the other hand, will become increasingly a factor. The obvious restrictions on promiscuous airport location in any area so limited in the number of possible airport sites as the larger cities indicate that an airport serving a large community is likely to assume many of the characteristics of a monopoly. It is apparent that the municipal airport will best serve the community only as long as equal treatment for all legitimate aviation interests is assured. The degree to which leasing the municipal airport to private interests will interfere with such control is a factor worthy of serious consideration.

CURRENT PRACTICE

There are relatively few municipal airports operated by private interests under lease, and still fewer commercial airports so operated. Of the forty-seven municipal airports from which data for this study were derived, only seven had been leased to private operators.[2] Rarely has a city offered its airport for sale.

It is claimed that a trend toward municipal ownership and private operation exists, but it is difficult to find evidence to support this. Yet with the decreasing need for the indirect subsidy afforded by municipal airport ownership and operation, the development of such a tendency may well be expected.

ORGANIZATION FOR AIRPORT MANAGEMENT

The scope and character of airport organization and personnel depend on the extent and variety of the airport's activities and the number of functions assumed directly by the operator.

THE AIRPORT MANAGER

The Airport Manager furnishes the connecting link between the administration and actual field operations. His title varies, sometimes being director of aeronautics,[3] or airport foreman, but, more generally, airport manager.

---

[1] Reference should be made to the following chapter on Fiscal Policy for a more complete discussion of other important financial factors which should be considered in relation to this question.

[2] See Appendix 32, Cities which Lease Their Airport for Private Operation.

[3] For description of the duties of a Director of Aeronautics, see p. 55.

Only a few cities have established specific qualifications which must be met by a candidate for this position. These usually require that the candidate be a licensed pilot and a graduate of a technical college. In Michigan a state airport manager's license is required, issued by the state Aeronautics Commission. At approximately one-third of the municipal airports studied, the manager was required to take a civil service examination. At the others no formal requirements had been established. It is popularly supposed that all airport managers are or have been licensed pilots. This was found to be the case at only a third of the ports visited.

Methods of selection and appointment were found to be as varied as are municipal charters. In most cases due consideration of merit was given, and a tendency evinced to make the position at least semi-permanent.

Managers at the municipal airports visited are paid from $1000 to $12,500 a year, the average salary being $3285 and the median $2500. In a few cases the airport manager is provided with an automobile, a house, or both, in addition to his salary. He is rarely permitted to engage in profitable operations on his own behalf at the airport. Only when his duties also include management of the local operating company is this permitted. An arrangement of this sort is dictated by economy and is usually found to be unsatisfactory both to the city and to the individual.

Salaries of commercial airport managers are higher, on the average, than those paid at municipal ports, due to the fact that at the former the duties usually include operating a school, a taxi service, or other services, as well as the airport.

The duties of the airport manager are many and exacting. He is the active representative of the city's aeronautical interests: the connecting link between the airport and the city, state, and federal governments, between the airport and the manufacturers and operators who use it, and between the airport and the public. He must formulate details of fiscal policy, secure new business, recommend and enforce field rules and regulations, make provision for handling spectators and passengers, see that the airport is adequately policed, and that airplane and automobile traffic are regulated. The variety of his possible activities is so great that a complete list of his duties would be lengthy indeed.

THE ASSISTANT MANAGER

In most cases airport activity does not yet justify the appointment of an assistant manager, although a number of the larger municipal

ORGANIZATION CHART DETROIT · MICH · MUNICIPAL AIRPORT

COMMISSIONER OF PUBLIC WORKS

CITY ENGINEER

ENGINEER MANAGER
SALARY $6000
AIRPORTS DIVISION
CITY ENGINEER'S OFFICE

ASSISTANT MANAGER
FUTURE

ADMINISTRATION

CHIEF CLERK & METEOROLOGIST
RECORDS AND ACCOUNTS
WEATHER REPORTS & RECORDS
SALARY $3000

SR STENOGRAPHER
CORRESPONDENCE · FILES ·
TELEPHONE SWITCHBOARD ·
INFORMATION
SALARY $1860

FIELD OPERATIONS

FIELD SUPERINTENDENT
AIR TRAFFIC · GROUND TRAFFIC
TAKE-OFFS · LANDINGS
LIGHTING SIGNALS
CONTROL OF SPECTATORS
SALARY $3000

FIELD CLERK
MEET ALL PLANES · NOTE RE-
QUIREMENTS · VOLUNTEER
INFORMATION · GUIDE TO VISIT.
TWO SHIFTS   SALARY $2400

DISPATCHER
OPERATE ALL CONTROL DEVICES
FROM CONTROL TOWER
THREE SHIFTS   SALARY $2400

HANGAR SERVICE

HANGAR SUPERINTENDENT
LICENSED AIRPLANE & ENGINE
MECHANIC
GENERAL SUPERVISION of HANGAR
INSPECTION & EMERGENCY REPAIR
SALARY $3000

GASOLINE ATTENDANT
3 SHIFTS   75¢ PER HR
OIL ATTENDANT
2 SHIFTS   75¢ PER HR
HELPER
2 SHIFTS   50¢ PER HR
HOSTLER   50¢ PER HR
JANITOR   50¢ PER HR
WATCHMAN   50¢ PER HR

PLANT MAINTENANCE

TO BE PERFORMED
BY
D. P. W.
CONSTRUCTION
DIVISION
AS REQUIRED
AND AS REQUESTED

66

and commercial airports have found it necessary to make such appointments. The Assistant Manager, as second in command, should possess the qualities of the successful manager. It is desirable that he be a pilot if the manager is not. The actual qualifications imposed for the position and the methods of selection and appointment are similar to those for the manager. In no case, however, was it found that the airport manager had the authority to select his assistant. The duties of the assistant manager are obvious. He should relieve the manager of much of the routine work and be capable of managing the airport alone during those times when his superior must represent the city elsewhere. At those municipal airports visited the assistant manager was paid a salary ranging from $1200 to $4500 a year, averaging $2201 with a median of $2000.

THE SUPERINTENDENT OF OPERATIONS

The position of Superintendent of Operations is commonly filled only at the larger commercial airports where operations are combined with airport management. Municipal airports do not operate air services of their own, and only in the most active of these airports is such a position provided for.

It is almost universally agreed that the superintendent of operations should be a pilot. He is personally dealing with the operation of planes and the regulation of pilots. He must superintend the arrival and departure, the service, storage, and repair of the planes. He is in charge of the mechanics, the helpers, and the dispatchers. Consequently the experience of many hours in the air is essential to a sound knowledge and a thorough performance of his duties. The superintendent of operations at the municipal airports visited draws a salary ranging from $1000 to $3000 per annum, the average salary being $2112 and the median $2400.

THE FIELD SUPERINTENDENT

The duties of the Field Superintendent consist mainly of field processing, seeding, drainage, runway maintenance, grass cutting, planting, snow removal, control of spectators, and maintenance of equipment. He is consequently the liaison officer between the city engineering staff and the field foreman. Under his direction are the foreman, laborers, watchmen, and janitors. Since activity at municipal airports usually does not warrant the employment of both a superintendent of operations and a field superintendent, the latter, aided perhaps by a hangar superintendent, performs the duties of both positions. This is the case in ninety per cent of the municipal airports visited. Qualifications for a field superintendent should include some training in engineering, and if possible, experience in flying. Salaries for this position at the municipal airports visited vary between $600 and $2400. The average salary observed was $1640 and the median $2200.

THE CHIEF CLERK

Another important minor official in the airport organization is the Chief Clerk, who is usually a civil service appointee. On his shoulders falls the burden of keeping the books and accounts, attending to correspondence, payrolls, meteorological records, permits, construction records, charts and maps, and of supervising the staff of clerks, stenographers, and telephone operators. In many cases there is so little clerical work that it may be done by one stenographer, while in others the chief clerk shares with the manager the duties of the assistant manager, superintendent of operations, and field superintendent. His salary was found to range from $1000 to $3000 with an average of $1916 and a median of $1800.

MINOR EMPLOYEES

The number of minor employees varies greatly with the size of the airport and the season. An average drawn from forty-seven municipal airports discloses eight minor employees drawing an average annual salary of $2000 each. The usual staff was found to consist of three laborers, one mechanic, one helper, one clerk or stenographer, one janitor, and one watchman. The wages of field foremen average $1950 a year, chief mechanics $2200, mechanics $2000, and helpers, clerks, stenographers, laborers, and janitors between $1250 and $2000, depending on the section of the country and labor conditions.

FUNCTIONS OF AIRPORT MANAGEMENT

When the necessary physical features of the airport have been completed there fall upon the airport operator certain functions necessary to insure the safe, orderly, and efficient use of the facilities which have been provided.

PROVISIONS FOR ORDER AND SAFETY

In addition to assigning a policeman or two to the airport many cities find it convenient for the county to deputize the airport manager and several of his staff, that state and federal legislation as well as local ordinances and field rules may be enforced.

Close attention should be given to the problem of handling crowds and a large volume of automobile traffic. Restricted areas for both spectators and motor vehicles should be established and adequate fencing and warning and direction signs erected.

FIELD RULES AND AERONAUTICAL LAWS

The enforcement of aeronautical legislation is one of the most important functions of airport management from the standpoint of safe and orderly use of the field. That section of the Air Commerce Regulations dealing with Air Traffic Rules is applicable everywhere in the United States; the remaining regulations apply only to planes and pilots engaged in interstate flying.[1] Thirty-five states have incorporated these model regulations in their own air laws. Other special state aeronautical legislation must be enforced.

Finally there are the airport's own field regulations. The Department of Commerce has formulated a model set of regulations which serve as a guide to the airport operator.[2] These are designed to control such activities as landing and taking off, taxiing, running engines, flight instruction and test flights, parking and mooring areas, dead lines, and fire protection.

Because of the wide flying range of the airplane it is apparent that, for the sake of safety and convenience, airport field rules as well as state aeronautical legislation should be as uniform as possible throughout the country. One need only refer to the complexities of state and municipal motor vehicle legislation to appreciate the value of attaining at least basic uniformity in flying and ground rules before a parallel condition develops as aviation activity increases. A few airports have adopted the Department of Commerce model field rules. Others have modeled their rules on these, while still others have largely neglected to modernize their local regulations to bring them into basic uniformity with the generally accepted standards established by the Department.

AIR TRAFFIC CONTROL

At a majority of airports air traffic has not yet become sufficiently heavy to necessitate control measures beyond the ordinary field rules

[1] "Airport Management," U. S. Dept. of Commerce, Aeronautics Branch, Aeronautics Bulletin No. 17.

[2] "Suggested City or County Aeronautics Ordinance and Uniform Field Rules for Airports," U. S. Dept. of Commerce, Aeronautics Branch, Aeronautics Bulletin No. 20, Oct. 1, 1929.

and Department of Commerce Air Traffic Rules, supplemented as need arises by oral directions to pilots. At the more active ports, however, a positive, controlled system of directing traffic has become essential.

The most commonly used device for such control is the siren. This is used to clear the field until the mail or scheduled passenger plane has landed or taken off. One long blast is the usual signal to suspend the use of the field for all other craft until two short blasts are sounded, when general flying operations may be resumed in safety. The siren has other important uses, such as signaling fires or other emergencies.

Another method of handling the traffic is by a flagman stationed at the end of the runway in use, who controls the movement of planes either at the signal of a director in the control tower or according to his own judgment. Two flags are commonly used. A black and white checkered flag is the "Go" signal. Red is the "Stop" signal for all planes: those upon the runway in use, those approaching the runway, and those intending to land. Both flag and siren systems are in use at many airports.

In some of the larger ports a complete lighting switchboard is installed in the control tower. By operating the approach lights, landing directions can be indicated at night. An illuminated wind tee is also used for this purpose. The Wayne County and Grosse Ile airports have installed an elaborate system of runway lighting. In each runway at the Wayne County airport lights are set in the form of a double-headed arrow, which can be made to point in either direction at the will of the man in the control tower.

Two-way radio communication as a traffic control feature has not been used extensively. At present its important use is to establish contact with a plane while in flight from one airport to another, rather than as a means of controlling traffic at the airport.

The assignment of certain portions of the airport for certain classes of flying is another element of traffic control. Some airports have excluded school flights and factory testing. A few of these permit the school base to be located at the airport, requiring that planes be flown off the field and back by instructors, and that the students do their flying and practice landing elsewhere. Other airports have developed adjoining property for school purposes. The latter solution, while relieving traffic congestion on the ground, does little to improve conditions in the air because of the proximity of the two fields.

Congestion of air traffic on and above the airport is increasing, and it is a necessary and proper function of management to provide adequate control.

WEATHER INFORMATION

The greatest aviation hazard yet to be conquered is weather. A major responsibility of airport management is the provision of adequate weather reports.

One source of this information is reports of observations taken at the airport. These should include such items as:

Height of ceiling	Barometric pressure
Wind direction	Humidity
Wind velocity	Temperature
Rainfall	

This necessitates the maintenance and use of the following instruments.

Ceiling projector	Hydrograph
Wind direction and velocity	Sling psychrometer
apparatus	Standard thermometer
Rain gauge	Maximum and minimum
Mercurial barometer	thermometer
Barograph	Thermograph

Use should be made of the daily map service from first-order Weather Bureau stations and weather reports from upper-air stations. Such maps should be obtained daily and posted, together with reports from adjacent airports. Weather-control stations on civil airways are another important source of weather information. To benefit by their periodic broadcast, the airport should be equipped with a radio and loud speaker. This information [1] should be systematically tabulated and posted on the airport bulletin board.

FIRE PROTECTION

The management should provide and maintain adequate fire protection.

The general hazard of airplane hangars may be roughly compared to that of garages, but there are certain factors which may make airplanes slightly more hazardous to store than automobiles. Some of these factors are the following:

[1] "Airport Management," U. S. Dept. of Commerce, Aeronautics Branch, Aeronautics Bulletin No. 17, July 1, 1929. For more complete information on this subject, see Department of Commerce publications.

ORGANIZATION CHART
MILWAUKEE COUNTY AIRPORT, WISC.

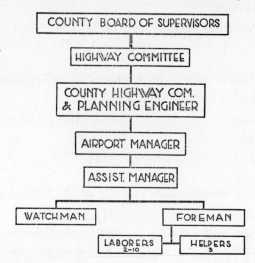

COUNTY BOARD OF SUPERVISORS

HIGHWAY COMMITTEE

COUNTY HIGHWAY COM. & PLANNING ENGINEER

AIRPORT MANAGER

ASSIST. MANAGER

WATCHMAN   FOREMAN

LABORERS 2-10   HELPERS 3

LOUISVILLE ·KY· MUNICIPAL AIRPORT

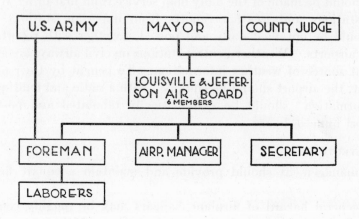

U.S. ARMY   MAYOR   COUNTY JUDGE

LOUISVILLE & JEFFERSON AIR BOARD 6 MEMBERS

FOREMAN   AIRP. MANAGER   SECRETARY

LABORERS

1. The combustibility of the airplane structure.

2. The presence of high-test gasoline in large volume.

3. The general refusal of pilots and mechanics to observe simple safety precautions in the handling of gasoline.

4. The usual lack of fire protection either in the form of first-aid fire appliances, water for hose streams, or fire department protection.[1]

The Aviation Committee of the National Fire Protection Association strongly recommends adoption of the fire regulations of the Department of Commerce model field rules.[2]

Large airports should "have a fire truck with first-aid fire appliances which is able to respond to fires in airplanes that may crash when landing. Most of the large city airports should provide such protection and the truck should be manned by one or more firemen at all times when there is any extensive flying going on."[3]

It is an unfortunate tendency at most airports to consider widely scattered first-aid fire appliances as sufficient fire protection, and to overlook the fact that these appliances are designed to cope only with relatively small fires, and should be supplemented by equipment of greater capacity.

MEDICAL ATTENTION

First-aid equipment should be instantly available. The type of equipment necessary for a Department of Commerce "A" rating includes

an ambulance, or some vehicle which can be used as an ambulance, equipped with the following: first-aid kit, drinking water, crowbar, wire cutters, hack saw, ax, cloth-cutting shears, fire extinguisher, two litters.

The first-aid kit shall contain at least 12 assorted bandages, 12 sterile dressings, 2 tourniquets, a supply of first-aid dressings for burns, adhesive tape, a supply of either tincture of iodine or mercurochrome, aromatic spirits of ammonia, and a paper or glass cup.

The litters should preferably be of the Stokes Navy type. If they are of the ordinary type, then the vehicle shall also carry an assortment of splints.[4]

[1] "Memorandum on Airplanes and Airports," by H. L. Bond, Engineer of the National Fire Protection Association. Boston, June 11, 1929 (mimeographed).

[2] "Suggested City or County Aeronautics Ordinance and Uniform Field Rules for Airports," U. S. Dept. of Commerce, Aeronautics Branch, Aeronautics Bulletin No. 20, pp. 8–10, Oct. 1, 1929.

[3] "Memorandum on Airplanes and Airports," p. 3. See footnote 1 above.

[4] "Airport Rating Regulations," U. S. Dept. of Commerce, Aeronautics Branch, Aeronautics Bulletin No. 16, p. 7, Jan. 1, 1929.

AIRPORT LIGHTING

Of the 453 municipal airports listed by the Department of Commerce at the close of 1929, 109 are equipped with beacon lights, and partial or full equipment for landing flood lights, flood-lighted buildings, boundary lights, danger lights, etc. Of the 495 private commercial airports, 71 are so listed.[1]

Any airport of importance must have adequate night lighting equipment. Such equipment must be supplied and maintained by the airport management, as convenience and safety demand central control.

The Department of Commerce Airport Rating Regulations list the following lighting equipment as necessary for an "A" rating:

> Airport beacon
> Illuminated wind-direction indicator
> Boundary lights
> Obstruction lights
> Hangar flood lights and roof marking
> Ceiling projector
> Landing area flood-light system

THE AIRPORT REGISTER

The Department of Commerce requires for an "A" rating that a register be maintained to include the following information:

1. License number and model of arriving or departing plane.
2. Owner of plane.
3. Pilot of plane and his license number.
4. Time of arrival and departure.
5. Number of crew.
6. Number of passengers.
7. Space for remarks covering any unusual situation.

The value of a careful tabulation of this information is obvious. It is as necessary to the sound management of an airport as is the record of the day's business to a commercial house.

> . . . It provides a valuable check on the movements of planes and pilots. It will assist in running down offenders of the air traffic rules and will protect innocent pilots who might be charged with some violation if they were not able to prove their movements definitely by an airport register. This is especially true along the borders where a more rigid check will have to be maintained than in the interior of the country.

[1] "Airports and Landing Fields," U. S. Dept. of Commerce, Aeronautics Branch, Aeronautics Bulletin No. 5, revised Jan. 1, 1930.

FLOODLIGHTS, MINES FIELD, LOS ANGELES

From the standpoint of the airport and the city, the register will be of value in furnishing data that may be of assistance in obtaining larger appropriations and a greater recognition of the work that is being accomplished.

In addition to the register provided for itinerant planes, it may prove advisable to work out a form for the use of the transport companies operating from the airport. This form would contain the information ordinarily recorded in the register, and would be furnished promptly by some one in authority in the transport company. It would save the time that would otherwise be consumed in traveling from the transport company hangar to the administration building upon the arrival or departure of any of the company's planes.[1]

THE AIRPORT BULLETIN BOARD, MAP FILES, DATA FILES

A bulletin board should be placed in a convenient and conspicuous place and the information on it kept up to date. This information should include:

1. Daily weather maps.
2. Weather conditions at neighboring airports, first-order Weather Bureau stations, upper-air stations, etc.
3. Airway notices regarding condition of intermediate fields, interruption of beacon service, etc.
4. Warnings of dangerous conditions at any of the neighboring airports.
5. Warnings regarding restricted areas in immediate vicinity.
6. Copy of local flying rules; copy of Federal air-traffic rules.
7. Location of fire-fighting equipment.
8. Statement of charges in effect at the airport.
9. Map of environs and information regarding various methods of ground transportation, charges, etc.
10. Notices involving any unusual situation that should be brought to the attention of the flying public.

The airport map files should contain the following:

1 complete set of airway strip maps
1 complete set of airway bulletins
1 magnetic declination map
1 large topographic map of the United States
1 map of each State in the Union
1 large scale local map showing highway connections, bus and trolley lines, railroads, etc.

In addition, the seaplane ports or landplane airports near the coast will need the following:

---

[1] "Airport Management," U. S. Dept. of Commerce, Aeronautics Branch, Aeronautics Bulletin No. 17, p. 7, July, 1929.

1 complete set of Notices to Aviators and Naval Air Pilot Notices, published by the Hydrographic office of the United States Navy.

A file of charts of near-by waters.

A file of pilot charts of the upper air, issued monthly by the Hydrographic Office of the United States Navy.

.　.　.　.　.　.　.　.　.　.　.　.　.

The following publications should be kept . . . [in the data files] and made available for reference purposes to those interested:

Department of Commerce Aeronautics bulletins.

File of Air Commerce Bulletin published by the Department of Commerce.

Copies of the principal trade journals.

Bulletins listing the reports of the National Advisory Committee for Aeronautics. This list can be obtained from the Superintendent of Documents, Government Printing Office, Washington, D.C.[1]

COMMUNICATION

Provision should be made at the airport for the acceptance of mail. Telephone communication should be installed. Arrangements should be made for the prompt dispatch and delivery of telegrams. The larger ports should be provided with a radio station. Eventually an airport of any importance will have available all these methods of communication.

TRANSPORTATION

Transportation is another problem which must be considered by the airport management. The service provided by air transport operators is not always sufficient. There are many who may have business at the airport who still may not be prospective transport passengers. The management should see that some service operating on a regular schedule at reasonably frequent intervals is available for transportation to and from the city. At present it is difficult for a person without an automobile to get to most airports quickly for a moderate sum.[2]

NEGOTIATING CONTRACTS, COLLECTING REVENUE, PROMOTING NEW BUSINESS

Proper functions of management include the negotiation of contracts, collection of revenues, and the promotion of new business. A policy

[1] "Airport Management," U. S. Dept. of Commerce, Aeronautics Branch, Aeronautics Bulletin No. 17, pp. 7–8, July 1, 1929.

[2] It is a common practice in aviation circles to refer to the distance from the center of the city to airports most notorious in this respect, in the terms of dollars of taxi fare.

of leasing land, buildings, and concessions must be drawn from the background of local conditions, so that it may best insure the steady progress of the airport toward its goal of service and profit.

One of the functions of good management is the promotion of activity at the airport as fast as safety and sound business judgment will allow. This promotion work may consist of air meets, exhibits, model plane contests, the preparation of interesting press releases, [and] the bringing of speakers to address gatherings on the subject of aeronautics. . . . In one sense the advancement of aviation is a question of selling, and it is the responsibility of everyone connected with it to help to develop interest and confidence on the part of the public. The individual airport will grow in proportion as the industry grows and any effort on behalf of the whole will be reflected in the fortunes of the unit.[1]

Some doubt exists concerning the efficacy of impressing the public with the safety of air transportation by means of air meets with their attendant thrills and possible mishaps. A well ordered and attractive airport at which transport planes arrive with impressive regularity, and where the needs of passengers are quickly taken care of, is more likely to impress spectators with the status of aviation than spectacular air meets. Thus sound promotion will consist of day-by-day demonstrations of efficient and safe management, and the enforcement of well drawn regulations.

MAINTENANCE

It is the duty of the management to maintain the airport in a state of cleanliness and repair. This calls for cutting grass in the landing areas, keeping up prepared runways, filling holes, providing proper warning signals to keep pilots off areas temporarily or permanently dangerous, keeping drainage lines and catch basins open, maintaining lighting equipment, keeping wind tees, wind cones, and similar devices in repair, painting and maintaining structures, and in general performing those numerous and petty tasks which promote a neat and attractive appearance as well as efficient and safe operation.

IMPROVEMENT

A sound plan for progressive and orderly improvement should be adopted and carried on as conditions permit. With the rapid growth of aviation, present facilities must be continually increased and expanded.

[1] "Airport Management," U. S. Dept. of Commerce, Aeronautics Branch, Aeronautics Bulletin No. 17, p. 9, July 1, 1929.

This will necessitate new grading, draining, clearing, surfacing, and construction and other general improvement to keep abreast of requirements.

CONTROL OF THE USE OF THE AIRPORT

The management must formulate sound policies for the control of operations. What financial and operating standards must be met by tenants? Will the number of transport companies using the port be limited? Will the number of taxi companies be limited? If so, will transient flyers be permitted to compete with them and on what basis? Will schools be limited or prohibited? Will factory testing be encouraged, restricted, or prohibited? Will private flying be permitted and on what terms? [1]

Both commercial and municipal airports solicit and encourage the business of air mail and transport companies, and make no attempt to restrict the number of such companies operating from their fields. A somewhat different policy is pursued in the case of taxi, charter trip, and "joy hop" companies. These three types of service are economically inseparable, and can be rendered profitably if competition is restricted on the basis of the volume of business available. Thus a majority of commercial airport operators reserve this type of business for themselves. The same practice is general in the case of schools, although the actual management of the services may be placed in the hands of a subsidiary or allied company.

The municipal airport, while less exclusive in policy, may also restrict the number of companies offering taxi, charter, and "joy hop" services. At most of the smaller municipal airports the financial condition of these companies and the limited business available usually succeed in effecting a high degree of automatic, if not formal, restriction.

The character and distribution of the various types of air services available at thirty commercial and forty-seven municipal airports is suggested by the following tables.

COMMERCIAL AIRPORTS

NUMBER OF AIRPORTS	NUMBER OF AIR MAIL COMPANIES
22	0
6	1
2	2

[1] For figures on type and extent of operations at airports visited, see Appendix 8. Rates and charges and the types of leases and financial stipulations they include are treated more fully in Chapter IV of this Report.

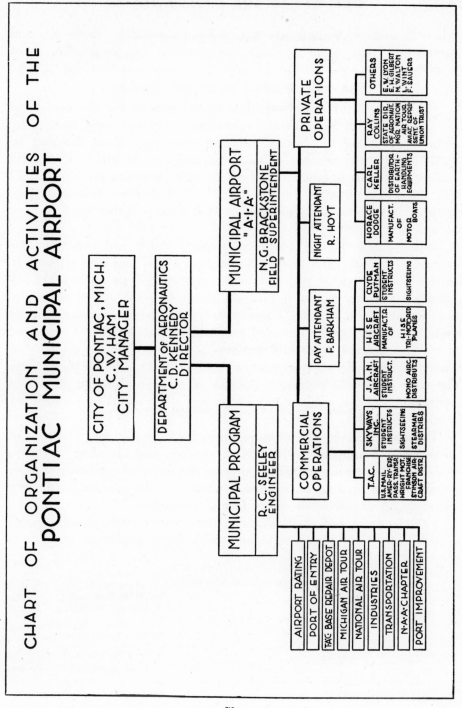

CHART OF ORGANIZATION AND ACTIVITIES OF THE
PONTIAC MUNICIPAL AIRPORT

CITY OF PONTIAC, MICH.
C. W. HAM
CITY MANAGER

DEPARTMENT OF AERONAUTICS
C. D. KENNEDY
DIRECTOR

MUNICIPAL AIRPORT
"A·I·A"
N. G. BRACKSTONE
FIELD SUPERINTENDENT

MUNICIPAL PROGRAM
R. C. SEELEY
ENGINEER

PRIVATE OPERATIONS

COMMERCIAL OPERATIONS

DAY ATTENDANT
F. BARKHAM

NIGHT ATTENDANT
R. HOYT

AIRPORT RATING
PORT OF ENTRY
T.A.C. BASE REPAIR DEPOT
MICHIGAN AIR TOUR
NATIONAL AIR TOUR
INDUSTRIES
TRANSPORTATION
N·A·A·CHAPTER
PORT IMPROVEMENT

T.A.C.
U.S. MAIL
AM GR.RY. EXP.
PASS. TRANSP.
WRIGHT MOT.
FRANCHISE
STINSON AIR-
CRAFT DISTR.

SKYWAYS INC.
STUDENT INSTRUCTS
SIGHTSEEING
STEARMAN DISTRIBS

J. A. N. AIRCRAFT
STUDENT INSTRUCT.
MONO AIRC. DISTRIBUTS

H. I. S. E AIRCRAFT
MANUFACT. OF
H. I. S. E TRI-MOTORD PLANES

CLYDE PUTMAN
STUDENT INSTRUCTS
SIGHTSEEING

HORACE DODGE
MANUFACT. OF MOTOR BOATS

CARL KELLER
DISTRIBUTOR OF EARTH- HANDLING EQUIPMENTS

RAY COLLINS
STATE DIR. OF AERONAUT.
MGR. NATION AIR TOUR
AVIAT. DEPRE- SENT OF UNION TRUST

OTHERS
E. W. LYON
E. H. GILBERT
M. WALTON
L. VINT
F. SAUERS

79

COMMERCIAL AIRPORTS — *Continued*

NUMBER OF AIRPORTS	NUMBER OF TRANSPORT COMPANIES
18	0
6	1
1	2
3	3
2	4

NUMBER OF AIRPORTS	NUMBER OF TAXI, ETC., SERVICES
1	0
24	1
2	2
1	3
1	6
1	10

NUMBER OF AIRPORTS	NUMBER OF SCHOOLS
1 (school prohibited)	0
27	1
1	3
1	5

NOTE. One airport allowed use of field as base only.

NUMBER OF AIRPORTS	NUMBER OF FACTORIES
22	0
4	1
2	2
1	3
1	6

MUNICIPAL AIRPORTS

NUMBER OF AIRPORTS	NUMBER OF AIR MAIL COMPANIES
16	0
25	1
2	2
2	3
1	5
1	6

Municipal Airports — *Continued*

NUMBER OF AIRPORTS		NUMBER OF TRANSPORT COMPANIES
21	. . . .	0
14	. . . .	1
3	. . . .	2
2	. . . .	3
1	. . . .	4
3	. . . .	5
3	. . . .	6

NUMBER OF AIRPORTS		NUMBER OF TAXI, ETC., SERVICES
3	. . . .	0
14	. . . .	1
10	. . . .	2
9	. . . .	3
2	. . . .	4
2	. . . .	5
1	. . . .	6
1	. . . .	7
1	. . . .	8
1	. . . .	10
3	. . . .	12 and over

NUMBER OF AIRPORTS		NUMBER OF SCHOOLS
5	. . . .	0
23	. . . .	1
8	. . . .	2
7	. . . .	3
1	. . . .	4
3	. . . .	5

NOTE.   One airport prohibits schools; two provide a practice field but have not developed it.

NUMBER OF AIRPORTS		NUMBER OF FACTORIES
27	. . . .	0
11	. . . .	1
8	. . . .	2
0	. . . .	3
1	. . . .	4

NOTE.   Factory testing was definitely prohibited at one airport visited.

Attempts have been made to exclude flying schools. Both the airport management and the school admit that such exclusion is logical and will eventually be common. At present the smaller schools cannot afford their own airports, nor can the airport management afford to ignore this source of possible revenue. One municipal airport which forbade school activities in the original draft of its regulations now proposes amendments in order to permit them. Other airports, both municipal and commercial, have limited the schools to the use of the airport as a base only. Some provide an adjacent field for students. Certain of the larger schools have, of course, provided their own airports, the use of which is limited to the school operations of the owners.

Prohibition of factory testing depends largely on local conditions. If the manufacturing interests are small, they cannot afford their own fields, and the amount of testing does not seriously menace the safety of other operations. If they are large, they may have their own fields. There are, however, several instances where airplane factories were the original reason for the location and the growth of the municipal airport. In other cases the location of factories at the airport has been encouraged. It is apparent, however, that as soon as the increase in air traffic warrants and the airport management can afford it, factory test flying will be generally relegated to its own fields.

PROVISION OF STORAGE ACCOMMODATIONS

The original storage accommodation was the right to "stake down" a plane in the open field. Some airports are not sufficiently equipped with hangars, and consequently many planes are still so accommodated. At most airports there now is sufficient hangar accommodation to provide for the usual demand. One airport prohibits "staking down" unless an unusual number of visitors causes an overflow. Another has increased its charges to discourage this practice. The provision of hangar space and such services as may go with it are optional functions with the management.

COMMERCIAL PORT PRACTICE

Practice as to storage accommodation at commercial airports varies. At six of those about which we have this kind of information the ground is leased and the hangars are constructed by the tenant under such structural and architectural restrictions as may be imposed. Four have erected all structures; four will lease either the building or the land;

Courtesy of Department of Airports, Los Angeles

COMBINED ADMINISTRATION BUILDING AND HANGAR, MINES FIELD, LOS ANGELES

sixteen have established no definite policy. The management at all commercial airports, however, provides storage accommodations for tenants.

MUNICIPAL PORT PRACTICE

Municipal airports are less likely to furnish all hangar accommodations than are commercial airports. The usual practice is the construction of one or two hangars by the municipality, which are operated for transient storage, unless the activity at the airport does not justify the reservation of so much space for that purpose. All municipal airports have constructed at least one hangar for this purpose. Twenty-one lease land to tenants, who have constructed their own hangars subject to varying structural and architectural restrictions. Eight municipal airports have built hangars and leased them. Two lease land or build the hangars according to the wishes of the tenant. At sixteen the activity is not sufficient to necessitate the adoption of a definite policy.

Provision for Fuel and Service

At commercial airports the management usually reserves the right either to sell all the gasoline and oil or handle all gasoline and oil sold to transients, or to grant these privileges to one or more oil companies. In most cases the airport management handles all such business. At a few this concession is leased to a single company.

At municipal airports the practice is much more varied. Of those studied, at 28 per cent it was found that the management handles all the gasoline and oil. At 23 per cent there are no restrictions. At 23 per cent the concession is leased by the management to one company. At 5 per cent it is leased on a flat rate to several companies. At 21 per cent anyone may sell gasoline and oil on payment of a specified tax per gallon.

SALE OF GAS AND OIL TO AUTOMOBILES

Thirty per cent of the airports studied sell gasoline and oil to automobiles. Most of the commercial airports sell directly, but in a few cases the concession is leased to a gasoline company. At the municipal airports the management uniformly leases the concession.

MECHANICAL SERVICE

Practice varies widely in the provision of mechanical service. The management at commercial airports has the equipment and personnel to repair transient planes and can reserve this business for itself. At municipal airports it is felt that the municipality should provide such service for the flying public.   Consequently an attempt is made to provide for repair work or at least to provide sufficient tools and facilities so that the transient may do it himself.

The demand for this service is not as yet sufficient at most airports to create much business.   All operating tenants of any size have their own repair shops, and if not overcrowded, are willing to do outside work. Since they are not required to render this service, and since it may be inconvenient for them to do so, it is wise for the airport management either to set up a general repair shop of its own, or to make special arrangements with a tenant having adequate repair facilities, in order to take care of the general flying public.

The Terminal Building

If the traffic justifies it, a pleasing, well equipped terminal building should be erected and maintained where passengers may comfortably await their planes, purchase their tickets, and enjoy other conveniences to which they are accustomed in railroad transportation.   The terminal is usually provided by the management, but may be operated by a tenant or a special company created for the purpose.   Portions of the building are reserved for office space.   The building should be located where it is most convenient for planes to receive and discharge passengers.   Four municipal and four commercial airports have constructed handsome buildings which combine the terminal with the administration offices. Centralization of administration and operation makes for order, safety, and convenience, and it is only a matter of time before all airports will be so equipped.

Eight municipal and two commercial airports have found it necessary to combine the waiting room, administration offices, and control tower with a hangar.   Such an arrangement, while convenient and often economically necessary, is at best temporary.   It adds to the fire hazard and has many other obvious disadvantages.   It is similar in principle to combining the railroad station with the roundhouse.   Fourteen municipal and six commercial airports have constructed permanent buildings to house the administration offices, but have made no special provision for passengers.   At five municipal and thirteen commercial airports offices are temporarily housed in one-story frame buildings. At sixteen municipal and five commercial airports the administration offices are installed in hangars.

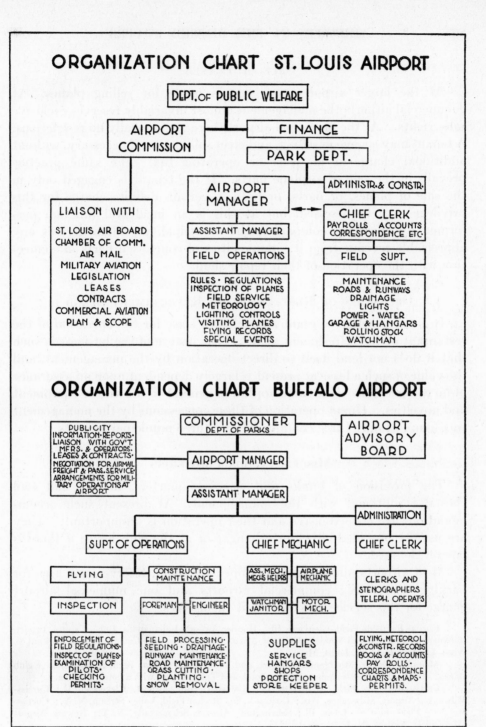

ORGANIZATION CHART ST. LOUIS AIRPORT

DEPT. OF PUBLIC WELFARE

AIRPORT COMMISSION

FINANCE
PARK DEPT.

AIRPORT MANAGER

ADMINISTR. & CONSTR.

LIAISON WITH

ST. LOUIS AIR BOARD
CHAMBER OF COMM.
AIR MAIL
MILITARY AVIATION
LEGISLATION
LEASES
CONTRACTS
COMMERCIAL AVIATION
PLAN & SCOPE

ASSISTANT MANAGER

CHIEF CLERK
PAYROLLS   ACCOUNTS
CORRESPONDENCE ETC.

FIELD OPERATIONS

FIELD SUPT.

RULES · REGULATIONS
INSPECTION OF PLANES
FIELD SERVICE
METEOROLOGY
LIGHTING CONTROLS
VISITING PLANES
FLYING RECORDS
SPECIAL EVENTS

MAINTENANCE
ROADS & RUNWAYS
DRAINAGE
LIGHTS
POWER · WATER
GARAGE & HANGARS
ROLLING STOCK
WATCHMAN

ORGANIZATION CHART BUFFALO AIRPORT

PUBLICITY
INFORMATION · REPORTS ·
LIAISON WITH GOV'T.
MFRS. & OPERATORS.
LEASES & CONTRACTS ·
NEGOTIATION FOR AIRMAIL
FREIGHT & PASS. SERVICE ·
ARRANGEMENTS FOR MILI-
TARY OPERATIONS AT
AIRPORT

COMMISSIONER
DEPT. OF PARKS

AIRPORT ADVISORY BOARD

AIRPORT MANAGER

ASSISTANT MANAGER

ADMINISTRATION

SUPT. OF OPERATIONS

CHIEF MECHANIC

CHIEF CLERK

FLYING

CONSTRUCTION MAINTENANCE

ASS. MECH.
MECHS HELPRS

AIRPLANE MECHANIC

CLERKS AND
STENOGRAPHERS
TELEPH. OPERAT'S

INSPECTION

FOREMAN — ENGINEER

WATCHMAN
JANITOR

MOTOR MECH.

ENFORCEMENT OF
FIELD REGULATIONS ·
INSPECT. OF PLANES ·
EXAMINATION OF
PILOTS ·
CHECKING
PERMITS ·

FIELD PROCESSING ·
SEEDING · DRAINAGE ·
RUNWAY MAINTENANCE ·
ROAD MAINTENANCE ·
GRASS CUTTING ·
PLANTING ·
SNOW REMOVAL

SUPPLIES
SERVICE
HANGARS
SHOPS
PROTECTION
STORE KEEPER

FLYING, METEOROL.
& CONSTR. RECORDS
BOOKS & ACCOUNTS
PAY ROLLS ·
CORRESPONDENCE
CHARTS & MAPS ·
PERMITS.

SALE OF PLANES

At the larger airports provision is made for selling planes. At commercial airports the management almost invariably reserves exclusive sales rights. At the municipal airport there are generally no restrictions. A tenant may engage in selling, and erect sales rooms if necessary, without additional charge in his lease or operating tax. The same practice prevails in the sale of airplane parts. If the tenant is engaged only in the sale of planes, or parts, or both, a certain definite charge for this privilege may be assessed, but as this is an incidental function performed by operating companies, the municipality seldom derives any appreciable revenue from it. Some cities of course sell parts in connection with the operation of their repair shop.

OPERATION OF RESTAURANT OR REFRESHMENT STAND

It is the practice to grant an exclusive lease for the operation of the restaurant or the refreshment stand. The nature of the business is such that it does not lend itself to direct operation by the management, and the value of such a lease at present is largely dependent upon an assurance of no competition. The same applies in general to the sale of equipment and novelties. Direct operation of these concessions by the management was found at only three commercial and three municipal airports.[1]

MISCELLANEOUS PROVISIONS

The provision of bunks and sleeping quarters, lockers and tool chests, is optional with the management. At present such accommodations are not extensive and their operation is unimportant. They are usually provided either in a hangar or at the club house if there is one on the field.[2]

Most airports, unless badly cramped for room, reserve some area for parking space. Six commercial airports and one municipal airport charge for this service and operate it themselves.[3]

[1] Curtiss-Reynolds Field, Glenview, Ill.; Hoosier Airport, Indianapolis, Ind.; Capitol Airport, Indianapolis, Ind.; Miami Municipal Airport, Miami, Fla.; Milwaukee County Airport, Milwaukee, Wis.; Lambert Field, St. Louis, Mo.

[2] Memphis Airport, Montgomery Airport, and Toney Field at Pine Bluff, Arkansas, have club houses. Oakland Airport is equipped with a hotel, and Tulsa Airport with a hotel for pilots.

[3] Curtiss-Reynolds Field, Glenview, Ill.; Curtiss-Herrick Airport, Cleveland, O.; Curtiss-Milwaukee Airport, Milwaukee, Wis.; Curtiss-Valley Stream Field, Valley Stream, N. Y.; Curtiss-Steinberg Field, East St. Louis, Ill.; Schenectady Airport, Schenectady, N. Y.; Newark Airport (Municipal), Newark, N. J.

Secondary Services

There are various extra-aeronautical services which may be operated by the management or leased as concessions. Some add to the convenience of the airport, some are important merely as possible sources of revenue. The following is a partial list of possibilities:

Hotel	Bowling alley
Swimming pool	Pool and billiard room
Airplane show room	Shooting gallery
Sale of novelties	Putting green for practice golf
Slot machines	Various stores and shops
Vending machines	

The actual use and location of the airport will determine to some measure the type of primary and secondary services rendered. Three commercial airports operate bathing beaches, two operate swimming pools, one offers moving pictures, dancing, and billiards, and another is equipped with tennis courts.

An attempt to emulate the functions of a park or an amusement center, however, is at best of doubtful value.

CHAPTER IV

FISCAL POLICY

WHAT does an airport cost? How can it be financed? What are the sources of revenue, and to what degree can they be counted on to pay operating expenses or produce a profitable return on the investment? What fiscal policies should govern the operation of the municipal airport as a public enterprise?

It is obviously impossible to return a specific answer to these questions. Little time has elapsed since airport management was put on a businesslike basis. There is as yet no standard system of airport accounting, nor any marked uniformity in management or operation. Consideration of the various items which influence cost, financing, and revenue in the light of the experience of representative airports throughout the United States throws some light, however, on problems of the individual airport.

Cost of the Airport Land

Purchase price of the land to be used for the airport is one of the largest items in the airport bill. It is apparent that the factors which influence the cost of land for any purpose exert the same effect on the price of land for airports. Proximity to the center of the city, location in regard to use zone, size of the city, the size of the tract desired, the number of available sites, the number of owners of the tract, and many more factors play their part in determining cost. The fact that the airport must necessarily be a large tract, that it must not be too many minutes distant from the heart of the city, and that the requirements of its location limit the number of possible sites are further elements which add to the cost of its purchase.

It is of interest to discover what the average cost of airport land has been throughout the country. At 45 airports, — 15 commercial and 30 municipal, — the average cost of the airport site was found to be $974.28 an acre. The average size of these areas was $396\frac{1}{3}$ acres.[1] The largest

[1] The average size of a total of 76 airports reporting on their total acreage was 338 acres.

88

investment in land amounted to $2,600,000; the smallest, $7500. The largest site was 1085 acres; the smallest, 100 acres. The cost per acre ranged from $6500 to $50.

It was found that condemnation proceedings made little or no difference in the cost of the land. In most cases condemnation proceedings were undertaken simply to clear the title after agreement had been reached on the price.

Commercial airports have in general paid somewhat more for their land than municipal airports, due perhaps to the fact that the sites of the commercial port are restricted to areas more likely to return immediate profit on operations.[1]

LAND OWNED OR DONATED

Four cities — Detroit, Jacksonville, Milwaukee, and Newark — have established their airports on land already owned by the city. This procedure avoids the necessity for a large portion of the initial cash outlay required for land purchase, but under certain conditions may be false economy.

Unless the site is well adapted to airport use, it is possible that the cost of improvements or the reduced efficiency and safety of operations arising from its location may ultimately raise the total cost of the airport above a figure required for the purchase of land better suited for airport purposes.

In several of the cities which have built their airport on such land the site could not be considered ideal. While these sites in general were found neither better nor worse than those purchased by a majority of cities, in every case better sites were available at sums which were not prohibitive.

In one city the site for two municipal airports had been donated.[2] The advantages of this method of land acquisition are obvious; the disadvantages are similar to those which are apt to be encountered when the land is already owned, plus the possibility of restrictions which may be imposed by the donor.

In every case, however, it is apparent that the requirements of an adequate airport site should not be lost sight of in an apparent saving in the price of the land.

[1] See Appendix 33, Average Cost of Land per Acre at 30 Municipal Airports and 15 Commercial Airports; and Appendix 34, Cost of Acreage and Number of Acres at 30 Municipal Airports.

[2] Miami Municipal Airport and Miami Dirigible Airport.

LEASING THE LAND

Leasing the airport site is a less common and often temporary means of acquisition. A number of reasons may make the purchase of the site either impractical or impossible. The necessary legal power to float a bond issue for this purpose may be lacking. The bonded indebtedness of the city may be so great that it would be unwise to increase it. A fair price for the issue might be difficult to obtain. The political factions in the city government may prevent the ordinance from passing the council. The issue might meet defeat in the hands of the electorate. If there is no possibility of financing the purchase of land, leasing is a temporary solution.

Lack of money is not the only factor which might make leasing the land desirable. A pressing demand for airport facilities, together with an inability to determine whether the immediate site is to be the ultimate one, may make leasing the proper solution until the question of site can be definitely determined. A few cities have adopted this procedure.[1]

It sometimes occurs that the one outstanding site cannot be acquired by any means other than leasing. This is often true when the land is owned by the federal government, board of education, or other public agency. One of the largest municipal airports in the country leases its land under such conditions, and the procedure has been followed in many cities.[2]

Of the airports studied, both municipal and commercial, 20 per cent leased their land. The yearly cost per acre at thirteen municipal airports varied from $5.00 to $192.18, the average cost being $40.09 per acre.[3]

The terms of the leases vary from three to twenty-five years, usually with provision for renewal for a similar period and with options to purchase at a fair price in almost all cases except where the land is owned by a governmental agency.

Cost of Improvements

The second big item on the airport bill is the cost of improvements.[4] These include clearing, grading, draining, surfacing, lighting, and structures.

[1] Des Moines, Tampa, Toledo.

[2] These cities include Albany, Boston, Chicago, Louisville, Ponca City, and San Francisco.

[3] See Appendix 35, Commercial Airports Which Lease Their Land, and Appendix 36, Municipalities Which Lease Land for Airport Sites.

[4] For more detailed figures, see Appendix 10.

CLEARING

The cost of clearing depends, of course, on the character of the land acquired. This cost was found to range from $0.99 to $501.54 per acre, with an average cost of $190.05 per acre.

GRADING

Another item which may vary greatly is grading. This cost varied from $6.51 to $9212.50 per acre with an average cost of $280.55 per acre. In every case the plans contemplated a maximum gradient of less than $2\frac{1}{2}$ per cent in the flying field.

DRAINING

Drainage still remains one of the major problems facing the airport engineer, varying with local conditions. The elevation of the land, the type of soil, the danger of floods, and climatic conditions may complicate the drainage problem and increase the cost of the airport. Various drainage systems are being tried throughout the country. At some of the most important airports careful data are being kept on the cost and efficiency of the methods in use. Time and experimentation should do much to simplify the problem.

At those airports which were meeting the drainage problem with some success it was found that from $2.50 to $1445.09 per acre was spent on this one item alone, with an average expenditure of $217.49 per acre.

SURFACING

The special preparation of the flying field includes seeding, and the construction of runways and taxi strips. The estimated cost of a good sod surface is about $200 an acre. The average airport is spending much less for this item. Runway construction is more expensive and at present the subject of much debate among airport engineers.

Possibilities range from an all-sod field to an all-paved field. If there is a good deal of flying activity, it is difficult to maintain an all-sod field. The cost of an all-paved field is at present prohibitive. Runway construction is an engineering problem, the costs and types of runways varying so widely that generalizations as to cost and merits are of little value.

LIGHTING

Flying is no longer confined to daylight hours. Scheduled night flying is increasing. At the end of 1929 there were 12,448 miles of lighted airways completed, and 1352 miles under construction.[1] Of the 453 municipal airports in 1929, 109 (or 24 per cent) were equipped with beacon lights or had partial or full equipment of flood lights for landing, flood-lighted buildings, boundary lights, danger lights, etc., and 71 (or 14 per cent) of the 495 commercial airports were so equipped.[2] Lighting is a definite item in the cost of the airport and all plans for future airport development make provision for it.

It is estimated that it costs from $15,000 to $20,000 to light an airport completely with beacon and boundary lights on a series circuit and with a 150-ampere arc flood light. Three shifts of personnel are necessary to operate and maintain lights, at a cost of $8000 to $9000 a year. Power bills and maintenance of lighting equipment, underground cable, arc mechanisms, etc., cost an additional average of $6000 a year.[3]

Figures obtained from thirty-seven lighted airports show an average expenditure of $16,935.58 for lighting equipment. The investment in each airport for lighting equipment ranged from $2500 to $65,000.

STRUCTURES

Utility and durability coupled with some architectural merit are factors in designing airport structures. They are required for the storage of planes, the housing of shop facilities, garage, administration offices, passenger waiting room, and restaurant. There are other possible needs, such as a club house or hotel.

All these facilities may be housed in a single structure or in several, according to the funds available and the amount of the activity. While the tenants may build many of the necessary structures themselves, the management must set aside a large sum for this purpose. Of those airports studied which were able to give accurate cost data on this item it was found that the municipalities were spending an average of $115,000 for this purpose, the commercial airports, $102,000, and the tenants at both types of airport an average of $80,107.96. The average investment for all structures was $143,417.53, ranging from $1000 to $960,000 per airport.

[1] U. S. Dept. of Commerce, Aeronautics Branch, Air Commerce Bulletin, Vol. I, No. 17, Mar. 1, 1930.

[2] "Airports and Landing Fields," U. S. Dept. of Commerce, Aeronautics Branch, Aeronautics Bulletin No. 5, Revised Jan. 1, 1930.

[3] "Airports as a City Problem," by Major J. E. Whitbeck. *Public Management*, Vol. XI, No. 3, p. 149, Mar., 1929.

Edgar B. Smith, Photographer

COMBINED PASSENGER TERMINAL AND HANGAR, WICHITA MUNICIPAL AIRPORT

SUMMARY OF IMPROVEMENT COSTS

The average cost of total improvements at seventy-three airports [1] was found to be $326,000. This figure does not truly represent the cost of an ideally adequate airport, which might well be more, unless the circumstances attendant on the purchase of the land and construction of the facilities were particularly favorable.

Bond Issues

Money for the purchase and improvement of land for municipal airports is usually obtained by a bond issue for this specific purpose, or by an issue for a general improvement program of which the airport is a part. The type of bond and the length of the issue depend on local practice and the market. Issuing and retiring bonds for airport purposes does not differ appreciably from issuing and retiring bonds for any other similar municipal enterprise, the principles of public finance applying with equal force. The average total amount issued for those cities studied which had financed their airports by issuing bonds was $976,287.50.

Appropriations

Bond issues have not usually been sufficient to cover the cost of the original improvements and subsequent development. A certain amount of capital outlay is necessary from year to year. Funds set aside for this purpose, into which the airport revenue is put, have been neither large nor numerous.

In some cases this money comes out of the amount budgeted to the department under which the airport is administered. Three cities have a special tax levy for airport purposes, the rate per capita being fixed by the legislature.

The amount appropriated often includes both annual capital expenditures and the amount expended to meet the operations deficit. Consequently it varies widely from city to city, depending on the size of the bond issue, if there was one, the improvement program, the policy of airport operation, and the financial condition of the municipality.

In connection with financing the airport, the unsound practice of putting the airport into some department, usually the park department, and letting the department use a portion of its regular funds for airport

[1] Some of these airports had little or no night lighting equipment and many had but one small hangar.

purposes was discovered in four cases. The airport suffered because sufficient funds for its adequate construction and operation were not available. The primary services rendered by the department were curtailed in exact proportion to the expenditure on the airport. Few departments have more money than they need, and placing an additional service of such importance as the provision and operation of airport facilities without adequate additional financial provision is poor economy.

FINANCING THE COMMERCIAL AIRPORT

The commercial airport is usually financed by the sale of stock. Sometimes the airport is not operated primarily as a commercial project, but is held and operated by a corporation of citizens to serve their municipality until the city can take it off their hands. In such cases stock is purchased by citizens in order to assist the enterprise, and with little or no expectation of profit.[1]

FINANCING THE COST OF OPERATION AND MAINTENANCE

The average operating and maintenance cost of thirty-one municipal airports where accurate data were available was $27,052.54 per year.[2] This sum does not include the purchase of items for sale at cost or profit, such as gasoline, oil, parts, etc. A little more than half of this sum is accounted for by salaries and wages, which averaged $15,700 and ranged from $2400 to $63,000.

Meeting the cost of operation and maintenance presents no unique problem at the commercial airport. The corporation engages in the business of operating an airport for a profit, or in a few cases at cost, and must eventually depend on revenues to meet the expense of operation and pay return on the investment. The municipality differs from the private corporation in that it need not operate its airport primarily for profit.

Considerable discrepancy exists at most municipal airports between operating expenses and revenue. Consequently cities have found it necessary to make annual appropriations for airport purposes.[2] A few cities have established an airport fund which is supplemented by appro-

---

[1] Those commercial airports visited which might be included in this category were: Charlotte Airport; Dayton Airport; Schenectady Airport; Toledo-Transcontinental Airport; and Tulsa Airport.

[2] See Appendix 37, Cost of Maintenance and Operation per Fiscal Year at Municipal Airports.

priations from the general fund when operating revenues fall below operating and maintenance costs.

At least one municipal airport makes no attempt to meet its costs from operating revenue. The policy is to charge at cost for special services, but to provide all necessary landing facilities free of charge, and to meet all expenses by funds raised through general taxation, on the theory that no charge is made for the use of the public streets, and that the primary function of the public airport is analogous to the function of the street.[1]

The majority of municipal airports attempt to derive as much revenue as possible without taxing the local operator too heavily, and usually entertain the hope that the airport will eventually become self-supporting. There is good reason for this hope. Municipalities attempt to operate their public utilities in such a manner that they will be self-supporting. The operation of the airport in many respects closely resembles the operation of a public utility.

It is generally conceded that similar enterprises should earn operating expenses of all kinds, depreciation allowance or reserve, interest on investment, emergency surplus, and taxes. There is some question whether earnings should also cover an allowance for sinking fund purposes, a reserve for extensions, and an accumulation over and above other items which may be drawn upon annually for general budget purposes.

There seems to be no reason why the municipal airport should not earn enough to provide for the first five items in the near future. If it is unable to do so in competition with a commercial airport in the same locality which is able to show such a return, there is good reason to doubt the advisability of continuing public operation of the airport. If no airport in the vicinity is able to show a return, nor has any prospect of doing so within a reasonable time after its establishment, then it would appear that there is not sufficient need to justify an airport.

Airport Earnings

Municipal airports do not show as profitable a balance sheet as do commercial airports. Their charges and the terms of their leases are far more favorable to the tenant than those of the commercial airports. The municipality can maintain a relatively low schedule of rates, and offer more favorable terms on its leases for land and structures on the

[1] For analogy, see p. 48.

subsidy theory and with a knowledge that deficits will be met from public funds. Several of the municipal airports studied showed a profit, but in terms of interest on the investment it did not exceed three per cent.

SOURCES OF REVENUE FROM AIRPORT OPERATION

The sources of airport revenue may be roughly divided into three classifications: charges for operations, charges for service, and income from concessions either leased or operated.

LANDING FEES AND PASSENGER TOLLS

A landing fee for transient planes is not usual at commercial airports. A landing fee for transport planes not using the port regularly is common, however. There is a possibility that a general charge for landings will be common in the future at such airports.

LEASING LAND OR BUILDINGS TO OPERATORS

One of the more lucrative sources of revenue is the leasing of land or hangars and other structures to the operators on the airport.

Land may be divided into regular plots and so leased, or it may be leased by the square foot or front foot. There seems to be no standard practice in this regard. The usual plot, however, runs from 100 × 100 feet to 350 × 225 feet. Taking an acre as a standard unit, the annual rental varies from $60 an acre to $5000 an acre, and averages $1010 an acre.

A sliding scale of rates is not uncommon. It is frequently the practice to increase the rental annually by a stipulated amount, also to decrease the price per square foot or other unit as the amount of land leased exceeds a specified minimum.

Leases vary from one to thirty years and include provisions for renewal. No standard manner of leasing airport land exists. Consequently no type of lease agreement can be accepted as entirely representative.

Most of such leases, however, include the following provisions:

1. Declaration of lease and description of property.
2. Length of lease, amount and time of payment, provisions for renewal.

3. Restriction of the use of the property; *i.e.*, to erect, maintain, and operate a hangar for airplanes, to teach aviation, to sell airplanes and parts, to store and repair airplanes, to keep and sell all necessary supplies, to repair parts for airplanes, and to do all incidental work.
4. Provision for the approval by the lessor of plans and specifications of structures erected.
5. Provision for the neat and orderly maintenance of the structures and property.
6. A clause prohibiting excavation or fencing of the property without consent of the lessor.
7. Provisions for fire protection.
8. A clause releasing the lessor from liability accruing from the erection of structures or use of the premises.
9. Provision for the payment of all taxes, assessments, license fees, etc.
10. Stipulations as to sub-leasing.
11. Provision for the restoration of the property to original condition at termination of agreement.
12. Provision for the carrying of fire and liability insurance by the tenant, the necessary amount of the insurance if collected going to the lessor in case the lessee defaults.
13. Provision by the tenant of a bond against liens.
14. Provisions as to operation; *i.e.*, only licensed pilots and mechanics, etc., to be employed by the tenant, etc.
15. Provisions for cancellation.
16. Provisions as to the removal of the tenant's structures at the termination of the agreement, and a stipulation as to the terms on which they will be taken over by the lessor.

Land leased for factory sites is divided into larger tracts and is usually offered at a much lower rate than that set aside for hangar construction. Such land is not as well located in regard to the flying field as are the sites reserved for hangars. At many municipal airports, as might be expected, the location of the factory is encouraged, and the return desired is an increase in employment in the city rather than a profit on the rental of land.

When the airport management erects the structures itself, the rental is figured as a percentage on the investment plus depreciation, taxes, and insurance, and calculated on the basis of square feet. The same type of rental applies to show rooms, offices, etc.

COMMERCIAL FEES

In order to induce operators to erect permanent and attractive structures, the management frequently releases them from the payment of the usual fees for commercial operation, provided a company's expenditure for a hangar or hangars exceeds the minimum amount stipulated in the lease. With this exception, at ninety per cent of the airports visited a charge over and above the lease is made for the exercise of the privileges of commercial operation.

Four types of rates are common: a charge per seat per plane, a charge based on percentage of the gross income of the operating company, a charge per passenger or per pound of mail and express carried, or a flat commercial rate.

Companies engaged in scheduled transport operation pay either a flat commercial rate or from 5 per cent to 10 per cent of gross income.

The Newark airport, the location of which insures considerable activity, and the policy of which is to be at least self-supporting, charges a fixed rate per passenger carried, and a fixed rate per pound of express and mail.

These charges are $1.00 per passenger and $0.01 per pound of mail or express carried in or out of the airport. Companies engaged in passenger hopping, scenic trips, and charter trips sometimes pay by passenger capacity. Rates for one-passenger and for twelve-or-more-passenger ships are as follows:

MONTHLY RATES

SUMMER		WINTER	
1 PASSENGER	12 PASSENGERS OR MORE	1 PASSENGER	12 PASSENGERS OR MORE
$8.75	$45.00	$7.50	$35.00
to	to	to	to
$18.75	$200.00	$22.50	$200.00

DAILY RATES

SUMMER		WINTER	
1 PASSENGER	12 PASSENGERS OR MORE	1 PASSENGER	12 PASSENGERS OR MORE
$3.50	$25.00	$3.50	$15.85
to	to	to	to
$7.50	$100.00	$7.50	$85.00

In other cases the rates are based on a percentage of gross income, varying from 5 per cent to 12½ per cent.

The flat yearly fee is also found. This charge is often $250 for the first two planes operated and $50 for each additional plane. Annual charges on the basis of passenger seats are usually fixed at $10 for the first seat and $5 for each succeeding seat.

Schools are taxed either on percentage of gross receipts or from 5 per cent to 10 per cent of each tuition fee paid. One airport charges the school a flat rate of $25 per student. An effort is made to separate income accruing from flying instruction from that derived from ground school operation and to tax only the former.

Photographic flying, if taxed at all, is taxed on a basis of percentage of gross income.

In an effort to protect their tenants and to discourage barnstorming, airports charge transient operators at a higher rate than they charge tenant operators. This charge is usually figured on the basis of a regular daily commercial charge plus the regular charge for overnight storage, whether or not the barnstorming pilot stores his plane at the field. In some cases the charge may be from 5 per cent to 10 per cent higher than the usual charge to tenants.

CHARGES FOR NIGHT LIGHTING

Charges for flood lighting are based on the cost of this service. For tenants the fee is usually either included in the lease or added to the commercial charge where the night lighting equipment is regularly used. Otherwise the charge is made by the hour or portion thereof.

The fee varies from $1 to $3 per hour and from $40 to $60 per month.

CHARGES FOR STORAGE

There is no uniform system of fixing storage rates. All ports attempt to apportion the cost according to the amount of space occupied, but use a variety of methods in determining this. The more common methods in practice are:

A flat rate based on the type and make of plane.
A rate varying with the seating capacity.
A rate varying with the number of engines.
A rate based on the number of linear feet of wing spread.

A rate based on the number of square feet occupied, the amount being estimated by calculating on a basis of twenty square feet for every linear foot of wing spread.

A rate based on the number of square feet occupied, calculated by the linear feet of the wing spread times the length of the fuselage.

(In all cases special consideration is given to high-wing monoplanes, folding-wing planes, or other special types.)

The last three methods of charging seem the most logical, the charge relating more accurately to the actual amount of space occupied.

Most commercial airports and a few municipal airports compute the construction and maintenance cost of the hangar per square foot of hangar space, and base storage charges on this cost, plus a slight addition to secure a fair return on the investment. This taxes the owner of the plane stored in direct proportion to the service and accommodations enjoyed.

The majority of municipal airports receive less than a fair return on their investment, due to basing their charges on what they feel the local operators can afford. A few airports, both municipal and commercial, copy their rates from their neighbors. The result is a number of different rate standards and a wide variation in the cost of the same unit of space, with little regard to the type of accommodation rendered.

If the storage charges are reduced to a common basis of 1000 square feet occupied, the rental for this space is found to vary from $35 to $85 a month, and from $1.50 to $5.50 a day.

Charges for "stake-down" privileges, where permitted, vary from $10 to $30 a month and from $0.50 to $4.00 a night.

CHARGES FOR SERVICE

Services may be supplied by the management, including washing, general servicing of the planes, repair work, and supplying of lockers, tool boxes, and bunks.

Mechanic's time is charged for at a rate varying from $1.50 to $10.00 per hour; helper's, from $0.50 to $1.50 per hour; washing planes, $1.25 an hour; lockers, $1.00 per month; tool boxes, $1.00 per month; and bunks, $1.00 per night and $15.00 per month.

Charge for lockers, tool boxes, bunks, etc., are based on cost and are not expected to yield a profit.

REVENUE FROM CONCESSIONS

Sources of revenue from concessions which the management may lease or operate itself are:

Sale of gasoline and oil to airplanes.
Sale of gasoline and oil to automobiles.
Sale of parts and accessories.
Sale of airplanes.
Restaurant.
Refreshment stand.
Airport hotel.
Parking privileges.

The sale of gasoline and oil is a lucrative source of income. Where controlled by the management it is often the largest revenue producer, particularly where there is a large amount of transient traffic. The profit varies with the airport. Some airports are able to realize as much as 11 cents a gallon on airplane gasoline, and 80 cents a gallon on oil. Gasoline and oil sales may be leased as a concession at a flat rate or on a percentage basis, varying from 5 per cent to $12\frac{1}{2}$ per cent of net income, or at a tax of from 1 cent to 3 cents a gallon of gasoline and 5 cents to 8 cents a gallon of oil. Another common method of deriving revenue from this source is to tax every gallon of gasoline and oil sold by the tenants.

The sale of gasoline to automobiles, if leased as a concession, yields the rental for the land and about 1 cent a gallon on gasoline and 5 cents a gallon on oil.

Servicing and repairing of planes and the sale of parts may be made to yield a nominal profit comparable to the income from similar services performed by garages.

Profit from the sale of planes is largely dependent on the market. The lease for the land or building and the charge for use of the field usually include this privilege.

The management of the earlier airports found it difficult to induce restaurant operators to set up in business at the airport. In order to have this convenience it was customary to offer the concession for a moderate fee on a long-term lease.

The present practice is to lease the concession on the basis of requiring a minimum guarantee plus from 5 per cent to 10 per cent of the gross income. In this manner the income derived depends on the value of the concession and does not unduly burden the lessee.   One commercial airport goes a step further and leases this concession for 50 per cent of the profits.   With the increase in activity at the average airport the restaurant concession has become an important source of revenue.

Until quite recently the airport hotel appeared to be an unreasonable investment.   At those few airports where a hotel, inn, or club house has been operated by the management or leased as a concession, it has been found to be a quite profitable venture, contributing as much as 10 per cent of the airport revenue.

Only at commercial airports is a charge made for parking.   Except when air meets are held, municipal airports, supported as they are by public funds, are not considered justified in levying such a charge.

Admission fees have the same status, and are even less common than parking fees.   Admission fees are usually $0.25 a person; parking fees, $0.50 a car.

THE LAW OF AIRPORTS

By

FRANK BACKUS WILLIAMS, A. M., LL. B.
of the New York Bar

INTRODUCTION

THE airport is an adjunct to flying, located upon the earth's surface. The law of the airport and of aviation generally is therefore partly the law of the air, partly the law of the earth. Aviation is a new thing in the world and the legal principles relating to it have by no means as yet been fully established. More nebulous in the air, more definite on the earth, this law is in process of rapid evolution. This report is an attempt to give in outline the present state of that law in so far as it is a necessary basis for the regulation and administration of airports.

AIR AND AIR SPACE

At this point the distinction should be indicated between air and air space. Of the air no one can claim jurisdiction or ownership; it passes freely from country to country, from landowner to landowner. It is with relation to the air space above the land of the landowner and the nation that questions of jurisdiction and ownership arise.

EMINENT DOMAIN AND POLICE POWER

In the establishment and conduct of airports and the passage of the aviator through the air space in approaching and leaving them are involved the taking of private property and the adjustment of rights of the public, the owner of the port, and the owners of the land over which the aviator flies. Rights in property under our constitutions and laws, when they cannot be obtained by contract, are acquired by virtue of the right of eminent domain with compensation; and conflicting rights in property are adjusted under what is known in this country as the police power, without payment. Some knowledge of the nature of these powers and the distinction between them is therefore necessary to the understanding of this paper. (38)[1]

[1] These figures refer to notes in the Appendix to this legal report which are numbered consecutively from 38 through 84. See pp. 176–185.

The broad line between taking and regulation is easy to indicate; to draw it, however, is much more difficult. Just and convenient as the distinction is, it cannot be claimed that, as stated in our law, it is scientific. Property is not a thing but a right, or rather a bundle of rights, in a thing. Our courts have always held that in order to be a taking, for which there must be compensation, an appropriation of all these rights is not necessary. Now regulation of a man's property — prohibiting him in some respect from doing with it what he otherwise would be free to do — is always the taking of a right in it. Nevertheless our judges as practical men recognize that the exercise of the police power — the power to regulate — is in accord with the provisions of our constitutions requiring compensation when property is taken. Most legislation is regulation. Such legislation without compensation was going on when our fathers drafted our constitutions, and they had no thought of forbidding it. The bases of this distinction have rarely been stated by our courts; instead they have been satisfied with placing the doubtful cases as they arose on one side or the other of the line dividing them. Perhaps therefore I may be permitted to quote a statement of the distinction which I have made elsewhere, especially since it now has the approval of one of our high courts. (39)

Difference Between Police Power and Eminent Domain

For a statute or other governmental act to be a valid exercise of the power of eminent domain or of the police power, it is evident from what has already been said that it must in either case tend to promote the public health, safety, morals or general welfare. What, then, is the line of difference between these two powers? The analysis of the cases seems to show that it is largely one of degree. Is it reasonable and proper, under all the circumstances, that the public good sought should be attained without compensation to those whose rights are to be limited to this end? If, on the whole, those affected are benefited by the measure, if the right surrendered can no longer, in the light of advancing public opinion, be retained in its fullness by its present possessor, if the sacrifice to him is slight or if the number affected is great, so that compensation is impracticable — in all such cases compensation is not provided for; otherwise the law demands it. In the decision, history, custom, opinion, as well as surrounding circumstances, play their part. (40)

CHAPTER I

JURISDICTION OVER AVIATION

NATIONAL (41)

BEFORE the recent war national and international air flight had begun. To justify these flights internationally two theories of the law on this subject were advanced. The first was that the high air, like the high seas, was not subject to ownership or sovereignty, but was of right free to the aircraft of all nations. The second theory was that the air space above the territory of each nation was more or less within the jurisdiction of the nation having sovereignty of the territory of that nation. To some extent this second theory was recognized by national legislation and international agreement before the war, in certain cases limiting and in certain cases allowing with greater freedom the passage over national territory of foreign aircraft.

With the war came the acceptance, by belligerents and neutrals alike, of the principle that each nation has full jurisdiction of the air space above its territory. This principle has prevailed ever since, the right of innocent passage being accorded foreign aircraft by international conventions and the legislative enactments of individual states.

FEDERAL

DIVISION OF POWER IN GENERAL BETWEEN NATION AND STATE

In the United States the full power of government is divided between the federal government and the governments of the individual states, these states having, by the federal constitution, ceded to the nation certain powers deemed to be of national scope, retaining for themselves the remaining powers. In the District of Columbia, the Territory of Alaska, the Canal Zone, and the Island Possessions, outside the limits of any state, the United States has full power, except as it has voluntarily delegated rights of self-government to these jurisdictions, as to a greater or less extent it has done.

BASIS OF FEDERAL JURISDICTION OVER AVIATION

The United States has no jurisdiction over the air, or the air space, above the lands and waters of the states as such. Its power to regulate aviation within the states, derived from the federal constitution, is based solely upon its control over interstate commerce. Other bases of the power have been suggested and discarded. Of these bases the admiralty jurisdiction was the one most generally urged; but this power, given the United States Government specifically over navigable waters, cannot be extended by mere analogy; and besides, the analogy between navigable air and navigable waters is most imperfect.

The United States also may set aside certain air spaces above states through which for military reasons it forbids aviators to go, and may use airplanes and establish air routes for the transmission of the mails, etc.; but these powers are not in any proper sense a power to regulate aviation as such. It therefore remains true that the only basis of such control is the right to regulate interstate commerce.

EXTENT OF CONTROL

Decisions with regard to the control over aviation which the United States has by virtue of its power to regulate interstate commerce are few; but evidently this power is in the main the same that prevails over movement by rail, ocean boat, bus, truck, or any other method of transportation. It is clear, therefore, that in general the central government may pass any regulation with regard to intrastate air commercial flight, or non-commercial flight, whether inter- or intrastate, which is necessary for the proper regulation of interstate commercial flight.

APPLICATIONS OF THESE PRINCIPLES

Planes and Pilots. Evidently, therefore, the United States may pass needful regulations to insure that planes are safely constructed and maintained and pilots skillful and reliable when in interstate commerce. This it has done by requiring such pilots and planes to be licensed, subjecting them to an examination for that purpose. On request it also licenses all suitable pilots and planes.

Planes and pilots in intrastate commercial and interstate and intrastate non-commercial flight are practically of necessity in the navigable air space traversed by planes and pilots in interstate commercial flight. Unsafe planes and unskillful or unreliable pilots in this air space are a danger to interstate commerce, whether themselves engaged in it or not.

It is clear, therefore, that the United States may regulate pilots and planes in flight for any purpose, but it has not as yet seen fit to do so except on request. On the same principle it is clear that the United States may prescribe the markings on all planes necessary for their identification, for whatever purpose used, in order to enforce its regulation of planes in interstate flight, and in fact it has done so.

Traffic Rules. Similarly the United States may prescribe traffic rules for all planes, in the air and in landing and taking off at airports and landing fields; and in fact it has done so.

Air Lanes, Beacon Lights, Emergency Landing Fields, etc. As aids to interstate commerce and as air mail routes the United States has the right to lay out air lanes or civil airways, with necessary beacon lights, emergency landing fields, and other facilities for flight; and in fact it has done so.

Transport Companies. The jurisdiction of the United States with regard to interstate commerce includes the power to regulate the individual or company engaged in interstate commerce. This jurisdiction in the case of railroads is in the main exercised by the Interstate Commerce Commission. It requires such a company, before beginning business, to obtain a certificate of convenience and necessity, and, if the service offered is not needed, it will not allow the company to proceed. The Commission also investigates the financial soundness of such a corporation, governs its financing, and within limits fixes its rates.

This jurisdiction has never by statute been extended to include aviation companies. For such an extension there are both advocates and opponents. The advocates point to the many mistakes made or abuses perpetrated by unregulated railroads in the early days. The opponents urge that we now have the most extensive and best railroad system in the world, which quite probably we might not have secured if in the early days of our inexperience we had attempted extensive regulation. The analogy to the aviation company is evident. These companies naturally oppose such regulation.

Airports. There is no doubt that the United States could own, operate, and regulate in considerable detail rail terminals in interstate commerce. It does not own or operate such terminals, nor does it regulate them in detail. Similarly it could, but does not, own or operate airports, nor, as a rule, regulate them. At one time the federal government owned a few airports, but it has now turned them over to the states or local governments within them.

Information. The United States collects and disseminates much information with regard to aeronautics, making use for this purpose of the Department of Commerce. Thus, without claiming any authority in this connection, it rates the different airports of the country and on request sends its representatives to aid states and local authorities in selecting sites for airports and in laying them out.

STATE

STATE JURISDICTION

Except for the power which by the United States Constitution it has surrendered to the nation, and the powers with which by state constitution or statute it has endowed the local governments within it, a state is sovereign within its limits. The state, except for the power to set aside certain air spaces for national purposes, has made no surrender to the national government of jurisdiction over the air space above it, as such, or of jurisdiction over aviation, except in the matter of interstate commerce. The state, therefore, on principles fully established with regard to transportation on land and water, has the right to control aviation as follows:

(1) It may pass additional regulations on matters which the United States has power to regulate, and has done so, provided the state regulations are not in conflict with those of the nation.

(2) It may in general regulate matters with relation to which the United States has regulatory power and has not exercised it at all.

(3) It may pass regulations with regard to matters over which the United States has no jurisdiction.

EXERCISE OF STATE JURISDICTION

And in fact the different states have enacted legislation and made rules along all the three lines above indicated.

Planes, Pilots, and Traffic Rules. Thus, for instance, the states have required pilots and the owners of planes in interstate commerce holding United States licenses to register with the state authorities; they have required all intrastate fliers and the owners of planes engaged in intrastate flight, for commerce or pleasure, to take out state licenses, as a rule exempting them from these requirements if they have voluntarily obtained United States licenses; and they have laid down traffic rules for fliers not engaged in interstate commerce, usually adopting the United States flying rules. Indeed, for uniformity, the state laws have in every way endeavored to make state flyers of all sorts take out federal licenses and follow United States traffic rules.

Transport Companies. The regulation of air transport companies — which the United States has not attempted — has been undertaken in a few of our states under general laws (42) or legislation especially applicable to aviation (43), and therein the states have been sustained by the courts. (44)

Airports. The application of these principles to airports is one of the main purposes of this report and will be found in the subsequent portions of it.

CHAPTER II

OWNERSHIP OF AIR SPACE, AND RIGHTS IN IT

The first part of this report has been devoted to a brief exposition of the law with relation to the jurisdiction of the air space and passage through it. Important in that connection and also with regard to the rest of this report are the questions of the ownership of that space and the nature of the right to traverse it. As to these questions it may be said in a word that this right of transit exists and will continue, but the nature and extent of the ownership of the air space and the right to pass through it are still unsettled.

UPPER AIR SPACE

"FREEDOM OF THE AIR," INTERNATIONAL

Ever since flying became common and the importance of aviation to mankind became clear, it has been evident that the aviator had the right to fly, or would be given that right. The earliest theory of this right was that it existed by virtue of the fact that the high air, like the high seas, being incapable of ownership, was not subject to the jurisdiction of any nation or the ownership of any person but was free for all to traverse. The air raids of the late war showed that jurisdictionally the analogy between the air and the sea was not tenable. No one any longer doubts that each nation has absolute sovereignty of the air space above it, that the aviator of one nation may fly above the lands and waters of another nation only by its permission, or that the permission will be granted generally by international convention or national law in time of peace.

"FREEDOM OF THE AIR," NATIONAL

Admitted to be untenable with relation to jurisdiction of the air space, the theory of "freedom of the air" is still advanced in the interest of aviation with regard to the ownership of that space. It is thus claimed in accordance with this theory that, limited only by the control which each nation has over the persons or things within it, the aviator may of

112

right traverse the higher air spaces because these spaces are not owned or capable of ownership or possession; that the only person who can claim to own these spaces is the owner of the land underneath; and it is absurd to say that his right extends between ever diverging lines from the convex surface of the earth to the farthest confines of space. Ownership, it is pointed out, is based on possession or the ability or interest to possess. It should be limited, it is said, to the air space which the landowner is using or may use; and he has no interest in the remoter spaces which the aviator traverses.

PRIVATE OWNERSHIP OF UPPER AIR SPACE

The view that the entire air space belongs to the owner of the land below it is an ancient one in the English common law; and that law, in so far as adapted to our circumstances, has become the common law of this country. This view is, as stated in the common-law maxim, *cujus est solum, ejus est usque ad coelum*. This maxim was taken by Coke (45) not from the Roman law, but from a gloss on that law. It is found in this and in a less extreme form in modern codes. Except as enacted in these codes, and even there perhaps with qualifications, it cannot be said necessarily to be the law. In our jurisprudence, based so largely on decided cases, it cannot be shown to be the law, for obviously until recent times no occasion could arise for deciding the point. The extent to which the older cases of invasion of the air space, at a much lower height, have established the principle is in debate (46), and the few modern cases (47) cannot be said to be conclusive. On authority, therefore, the question is still unsettled. (48)

TRESPASS AND NUISANCE

In our earlier common law a right was that of bringing one or more of a given number of specific actions; if no action could be found for a given injury, there was no redress. In that earlier law trespass lay for entry upon the real estate of another and damage was not a necessary element in the wrong. On the contrary, nuisance, an action arising later in the history of the law, was based upon damage and did not lie unless actual damage was done. An argument for the "freedom of the air" is that if the upper air space belongs to the landowner below, the aviator, traversing that space without damage to that landowner, nevertheless commits a trespass and may be enjoined from such flight or at least subjected to suits without end; so that the only method of allowing aviation to continue would be to take and pay for rights in all air spaces to be traversed, which would be practically impossible. A constitutional amendment was even suggested by a firm believer in the ownership of the air space *"usque ad coelum"* as the only way of making aviation in this country legally feasible.

CHANGE OF REMEDY

This argument for the private ownership of the air space would seem to be unsound. Under our constitutions a given legal remedy may without compensation be modified or taken away without being considered an illegal taking of property if a reasonable remedy for any substantial wrong suffered is left. If the landowner is actually damaged by transit at whatever height, through what, for the purposes of argument at this point, may be characterized as his air, an action for nuisance will lie and is an all-sufficient remedy; but if it is a mere trespass without damage, he may be constitutionally deprived of the right to sue for it. In some jurisdictions, also, under modern laws, there is no right to sue at all for an alleged injury for which damage is not suffered, the court considering all such suits frivolous; and there is no constitutional reason why this should not be made the law in all the states.

Other methods of obtaining the right to traverse the upper air, if privately owned, have been suggested. The United States, and the states in so far as possible without conflicting with the federal rights, have the power to aid and improve navigable waters, often inflicting substantial damage to land under water and riparian land in so doing. The power of the United States is based upon both the admiralty power and the right to foster interstate commerce. There is a certain analogy between navigable waters and navigable air. It must be remembered, however, that the law of navigable waters has a long history behind it which has shaped its development.

It has also been suggested that the United States, and the states in so far as compatible with the federal power, may grant the right to fly through the upper air under the police power as an adjustment of rights in the public interest; and for this claim there is already legal authority. (49) This is the use of the police power in a new field. That power, however, is not a fixed quantity, but changes from time to time to meet changed conditions of society; or, to speak more accurately, the power remains the same, its apparent extension being merely the application of the principle upon which it is based to new conditions as they arise. (50)

LOWER AIR SPACE

In the taking off and landing of planes at airports, at the customary angle of about seven to one, it is necessary to traverse the air spaces more immediately above land abutting on and in the neighborhood of the port. It is therefore the ownership of these spaces and the right of the aviator to go through them that are of concern to us in this inquiry; and the brief exposition of the law of aviation, including rights in the upper air space, is useful to us as a necessary introduction to a discussion of the law with regard to these lower air spaces.

COMMON-LAW RIGHTS

With regard to the rights of the owner of the land underneath and the aviator in these lower air spaces we find the same differences of opinion as with relation to the higher air spaces. It is admitted by all that the landowner may, in the absence of zoning and similar restrictions, build structures at any time for his use to any height he desires. It is maintained by some that this is the extent of the landholder's title, any further rights in the air spaces above him, like his rights with relation to uses on neighboring land, being those of not being disturbed or annoyed; so that the aviator may at all times traverse the air space not at that time used by the landowner subject only to the action of nuisance if he annoys that owner by so doing.

In support of the opposing theory that the landowner owns the air space above that part of it which he has ever occupied are cited cases of overhanging eaves, wires, etc., for which the landowner has always had his redress. (46, 47, 49) In answer it is pointed out that these uses may ripen into an easement depriving the owner of the right to occupy this space in the future, while the aviator, passing at intervals in no one fixed path, would acquire no easement. It would seem, however, that a constant stream of airplanes approaching or leaving an airport were moving with sufficient frequency and in a path sufficiently definite to be capable of obtaining an easement. Be this as it may it would seem to be good reasoning and established in principle by the older cases that the landowner does own the air space considerably beyond the limits of which he has taken actual possession. Of some pertinency in this connection is the fact that "Air rights" — *i.e.*, the right to have the air space above a contiguous building open — are in these times often sold by the owner of a low building or vacant lot to an adjacent landowner desirous of light and air over it for the benefit of the structure he is planning to erect. And there is one recent case (49), stating that the low flight of aviators over wild land, without physical injury to it or annoyance to its owner, is a trespass.

It appears probable, therefore, that the landowner has title to the air space above his land beyond the space which he has already taken possession of and is using. To what height that title goes it is difficult to indicate. Probably the height would differ with circumstances and change as those circumstances change. It is quite in consonance with this theory, of course, that he does own the upper air space used by the aviator who does not, at that point, descend toward an airport; or that he does not. The question of the ownership of the upper air spaces has been discussed above. At what height these upper spaces are at present thought to be may perhaps be indicated by the United States and state laws defining the rights of aviators in flight while they are not descending in their more immediate approach to port.

With the lower air spaces in private ownership it would seem nevertheless possible in several ways to give the aviator the right to traverse them; for, first, the landowner might be deprived of the right of action in the nature of trespass if left his action in the nature of nuisance. Second, the right to such approach might be given by the national or state use of the police power. A right obtained in either of these ways would not justify any undue disturbance of the landowner in the present reasonable use of his land or prevent him from changing that use. Third, and less probably, on the analogy of the air to the water, the right might be conferred, with or without substantial or permanent damage to the landowner, under the state or national jurisdiction over commerce, as an improvement of aerial navigation.

It has been intimated that the United States Air Commerce Act, 1926, in its provisions for take-off and landing at airports, does not authorize them but simply relieves them of their criminal character; but this is not an intimation that appropriate language could not be employed which would authorize them.

If the aviator had the right to traverse the air space at any altitude, high or low, by virtue of the police power, he would not obtain an easement, for the landowner could not prevent such passage. This is especially important in case the passage is at a height at which the landowner had not at that time occupied the space with buildings, but later might desire to do so.

CHAPTER III

AIRPORTS

ESTABLISHMENT

IN GENERAL

A Public Purpose. It is evident in principle that the establishment by a governmental agency of a public airport, as an aid to communication and commerce, is a public purpose; and the courts have so held. (51) Almost without exception the various state, territorial, and insular governments have been authorized by statute to establish such ports. (52) The statutes usually declare such establishment to be a public purpose. (53) Such a declaration is not essential to make it a public purpose, nor is it conclusive that it is such; but it does tend to that result, for one element in a public purpose is public opinion and public need, which is to some extent proved to exist by a solemn declaration to that effect by the people's legislature, speaking for it.

Airports not established by a public authority may, as already indicated, be divided into semi-public and strictly private ports. A company holding itself out to the public as a common carrier of persons or goods or both is a public utility, and the port owned and operated by it partakes of this public character. An aviation company transporting persons or goods or both for a single company, etc., is private, as is the port which it owns and uses.

Acquiring the Land. Whether or not the land for a public airport could be acquired by eminent domain by any given jurisdiction without special legislation depends upon the existing general condemnation laws applicable to that jurisdiction. There cannot be any doubt of the constitutionality of such a taking if duly authorized. The question whether the general law in any given case allows such a taking is no longer, however, of any great practical importance, since in nearly all jurisdictions authorizing airports there is specific authority to take land for them by eminent domain.

117

Upon satisfaction of any claims for damage caused thereby to neighboring landowners, the local authority may, of course, if it sees fit, close any highways preventing the acquisition of a suitable tract of land needed for its port and, if it seems best, unite the bed of the abandoned street with the rest of the tract.   (54)

Whether, having the power of eminent domain, a given jurisdiction instead of taking the entire interest in the land may merely lease it for a port, is again a question of the wording of the law invoked.   As a rule statutes authorizing taking for ports authorize the taking of either the fee or a leasehold interest.

There is no constitutional reason why semi-public aviation companies should not be given the power of eminent domain in the acquisition of airports, but as yet none of them has been granted this power.

Paying for the Land.   How, in the absence of special statutory provisions, a given jurisdiction authorized to acquire land for an airport may or shall pay for it, is again a question of general law.   As a rule there are now specific statutes of one sort or another in the various jurisdictions authorizing the incurring of indebtedness, the issuing of bonds, the levy of taxes, etc., and to some extent provisions for the financing of airports in special ways.

ESTABLISHMENT BY STATE

In a few states the state itself establishes airports directly or by means of a state board (55); in some cases it aids municipalities in establishing them.   (56)

ESTABLISHMENT BY LOCAL GOVERNMENTS

Without Special Statutory Authority.   As already indicated the entire authority of a state is in the state itself except as it has endowed local governments with some part of it.   More and more states are giving these governments large powers of self-government by constitutional amendment or by statute.   These provisions vary greatly in the different states. It is probable that in some of these states, "home rule" communities have the power, without special statutory grant, to establish and operate airports.   Any extensive consideration of "home rule," however, is beyond the scope of this inquiry.

Special Statutes.   The question whether particular local governments have the power without specific grant to establish airports is now of little practical importance.   It is to cities that broad powers have most extensively been given in the past; and these cities, as already indicated, in common with counties and other local governments, have very generally of late been granted the power specifically. (57)

AIRPORTS OUTSIDE LIMITS OF PUBLIC AUTHORITY ESTABLISHING THEM

As a rule a municipality authorized to engage in a given enterprise, acquire the necessary land, absolutely or by lease, by eminent domain and pay for it, has, within the state, the right to do so outside its municipal limits without special statutory authority to that effect; and this rule should hold with regard to airports. (58) In many cases municipalities are specifically empowered to do so. Counties, being larger and needing the power less, are less often given it. In three statutes the establishment of an airport outside the state was authorized. (59) Obviously one state has no right to exercise the power of condemnation in another, although that other state will sometimes provide for the employment of its power to that end.

There are statutes allowing municipalities to condemn land for many purposes, such as waterworks and parks; and in states in which aviation is held to be a park purpose land may be condemned for a park and used for an airport, thus establishing an airport outside municipal boundaries without specific authority to do so.

JOINT AIRPORTS

Without a grant of that power from the state two or more local governments do not have the right to engage in any enterprise jointly. In some states broad general powers of prosecution of joint enterprise have been given local governments. Statutes with regard to aviation often authorize local governments to establish and administer airports jointly. (60)

CORRELATION OF AIRPORTS AND RAILROADS

Corporations are limited to the powers conferred upon them by statute. Whether railroads and other land and water transportation companies could lawfully, in the absence of a specific grant of power from the state, make use of the airplane in their business could be determined only by an examination of their charters, and the statutes and rulings of public utility corporations relating to these older methods of conveyance. In a number of states, railroads are more specifically empowered to use the airplane. (61)

Within constitutional limits the right of the state or any of its local governments to use or acquire land already owned by it for any given purpose without special statutory authority to do so is dependent upon existing laws.   The extent of the general powers of local governments has already been indicated.

There are many statutes specifically authorizing the state or local government, without further payment or proceeding of any sort, to use for an airport land already owned by it.   In certain cases this would and in others would not seem to be constitutional.

When the public authority owns the entire title to land it may by general or special law be given the power to use land devoted to one public use for another public purpose.   As a rule there are limitations upon this right in the case of certain uses, such as parks, and none in others, such as sites for public buildings.   Thus a municipality if it is given the power to discontinue a park use is often required first to obtain approval for this step by referendum, but is allowed to sell a fire engine house site or use it for a police station without special formality or authority.

Under some condemnation laws a local government takes a fee, under others only an easement for the given purpose, and if only an easement has been acquired and the property is used for another purpose, it reverts to the former owner.   In either case the state has the power to authorize land condemned for one purpose to be condemned for another.

Where land is dedicated by the owner to the public for a given use, it cannot, except by condemnation, be used for another purpose; and if so used, it reverts to the former owner.   (62)

AIRPORTS IN PARKS

It seems clear on principle that use for an airport is not a park use.   A park is intended for recreation, an airport is a facility of business and commerce.   It has been held in one case (63), however, that an airport is a park use, because aviation is a sport and an amusement.   This, however, is a minor purpose and not the essential end and aim of aviation.

However, if a part of a park is devoted to the landing and taking off of pleasure planes or planes for access to the park for recreation, the land so used might well be held to be devoted to a park use.

There are a number of statutes authorizing the use of parks as airports.   (64)

If it be granted that use for an airport is not a park use, then conversion of a portion or all of a park into an airport would be legal only in so far as it is possible for a public authority to change the use of land already owned by it. In this connection it should be borne in mind that where a portion of a tract is dedicated as a park and other portions of it sold with this representation, the purchasers also have rights in the land dedicated as a park.

REGULATION OF LOCATION

BY LOCAL GOVERNMENT, THROUGH ZONING

In the absence of state control or local regulation, the public authority, public utility, or private corporation or individual with power to establish an airport within the limits of a given local government may select any site for it within its boundaries that it or he sees fit, taking the land for the purpose by eminent domain or private purchase as it or he may have the right to do. The method by which a public authority determines whether it shall engage in any given activity in which the state has given it the power to embark and what land it shall use, if it already owns it, or acquire, if it does not, for the purpose, varies of course in different local governments, sometimes being more or less subject to the action of a planning commission with regard to it.

If there is a zoning ordinance in force for the local government in question, it usually regulates only the territory within the limits of that government. The instances in which a municipality has power to pass zoning regulations to control land outside its limits in this country are so rare as to be negligible. (65) There are in a few jurisdictions regional zoning provisions.

In some cases the state, another local government, or the local government enacting the zoning ordinance is, by the terms of the state enabling act, and the local ordinance passed under it, bound by the ordinance as to the land situated within the local limits, and sometimes it is not so bound. In some cases the zoning ordinance exempts public utilities, more or less completely, or privileges them, leaving them to the control of public utility commissions as a substitute. The better method, perhaps, is to make all land within the local limits subject to the ordinance.

The difficulty in many cases in finding a site for an airport suitable for aviation is so great that it seems necessary to provide a method by which ports may be admitted into any zoning district. The possibility of injuring existing uses and hurting the future development of the district for other purposes, however, is manifest.   Zoning must be for the advantage of the community as a whole, and must deal justly with the interests of all.   The solution of this difficult situation is met in a majority of the zoning ordinances in this country by allowing airports to be located in any district on permission of the board of appeals, which always has power to impose conditions suitable to local circumstances to obviate damage and prevent injustice.   The disadvantage, felt by all students of zoning, of increasing the discretionary power of boards of appeals, may be lessened somewhat by giving the municipality the power to lay down rules with regard to airports, the same for all parts of the municipality but varying in different municipalities so as more closely to fit local circumstance.

REGULATION OF LOCATION BY STATE

In some cases the state selects by statute the site for an airport for its own use, for the use of the citizens of the state more or less as a whole, or for a particular community; in a few states there are state airport boards to make the selection.

Some of these boards are given the duty to license airports, no local community being permitted to lay out an airport until it has obtained such a license.   Obviously these boards can control the location of local airports.   (66)

REGULATION OF LOCATION BY COÖRDINATE ACTION

In many cases an airport is selected on the advice of the Department of Commerce after one or two short visits from its representative.   Great as is the knowledge and experience of this department, a port cannot safely be located on this general knowledge alone.   Such a selection is not only a matter of general but of great local importance, and should be carefully studied with expert assistance by the local planning commission in conjunction with the local zoning authorities, after which the national or state authorities should be called in; for it is only with a full understanding of the local situation obtained in some such way that outside experience has its full value.

TAXATION

As a rule in the absence of statutory or constitutional provisions on this subject the property of a municipal corporation where appropriated to public uses is exempt from general taxation or special assessment whether that property is located within or outside the limits of the municipality owning it. (67) There are many statutory and constitutional provisions in the different states subjecting to or exempting from taxation such property generally and in specific cases. A few such statutes have been passed with regard to airports. (68)

LIABILITY FOR NEGLIGENCE

An aviation company, whether a common carrier and therefore a public utility, or engaged in running a school, carrying passengers or freight for a single concern, etc., is of course liable for negligence in the conduct of its business. Whether or not a municipal corporation is so liable in the management of an airport is a matter of dispute. The general rule is that a municipality is liable for negligence in the prosecution of an enterprise if engaged in it in its corporate capacity but not if so engaged in its governmental capacity. The distinction is a confused one, in consequence of which the decisions are in conflict, with differing rules in different jurisdictions. In a case on this point with regard to airports it was held that the municipal corporation was liable. (69) There are statutes exempting public ports from liability. (70)

Accidents occasionally happen from the falling of the plane on abutting or neighboring property as the plane is leaving or approaching the port. In the absence of statute the aviation company or the aviator, or both, would be liable in such cases for negligence.

There is a doctrine, commonly referred to as *res ipsa loquitur*, that

Where the thing is shown to be under the management of the defendant or his servants, and the accident is such as in the ordinary course of things does not happen if those who have the management use proper care, it affords reasonable evidence in the absence of explanation by the defendants that the accident arose from lack of care. (71)

The doctrine has been applied to railroad cars and other means of public conveyance, elevators and other falling objects, and the failure of mechanical contrivances generally. It is urged against its application to the falling airplane that there are too many causes, such as wind or weather, other than negligent operation which may occasion the accident, for negligence to be presumed. On the other hand the doctrine is applied in many instances where the facts are necessarily known to the defendant and cannot be obtained by the plaintiff, which is peculiarly applicable to the falling plane. (72)

There are now many statutes with regard to the responsibility of the aviator for damage caused by him to the land beneath, some stating that he shall be liable only for negligence (73), others holding him absolutely liable for any damage, whether negligent or not.   (74)

INSURANCE

Most important in the conduct of any branch of business in these days, to the industry, to those served by it, and to those having business relation to it, is insurance.   There are now many cases specifically dealing with the liability of the aviation company to those whom it carries and those whose goods it transports.   There are also cases with regard to the liability of such company to its employees.   These cases, which are rapidly growing in number, may be found without difficulty in the law digests.   The cases with regard to other methods of transport are also in print.   The subject has also been dealt with, in many ways, by statutes expressly related to aviation.   (75)

NEIGHBORING PROPERTY

PROTECTION OF GENERAL PUBLIC, AIRPORT, AND NEIGHBORING PROPERTY

In the location and operation of an airport are involved the general interest of the public in an undertaking which promotes the general welfare, and the more special interests of the owner and operator of the port and of abutting and neighboring landowners.   The public authorities, state or local, in control in this matter may be and often are the owners and operators of the port; it is nevertheless their duty, while aiding the port in all proper ways, to deal justly with the local interests to a greater or less degree conflicting.   The same considerations apply to a port owned and operated by a public utility corporation, and to some extent to a private port.

The observance of this policy is especially necessary in the location of the port.   It is essential that the port should be placed so as to be convenient and safe of access to the aviator and so as to serve the public.   The choice of locations is often limited.   Nevertheless it should be remembered both that an airport is sometimes an injury to surrounding property, and that the uses of surrounding property are often a difficulty in the operation of the port if they are allowed to remain or an expense if they are limited or abolished.   The avoidance of conflict between airport and other local uses, in so far as it can be attained in the location of the port, is consequently of advantage to all interests, general and special.

A conflict of interests, however, cannot in all cases be avoided. A statement of the rights and duties of the port on the one hand and of the surrounding landowners on the other is, therefore, necessary.

PROTECTION OF PORT

Nature of Surrounding Land. Viewed with relation to the lands surrounding them, ports may be described as follows: the port on expensive land on the whole intensively developed with residences, business, or industry; the port surrounded by land less intensively developed, and generally residential; and the port in a neighborhood practically undeveloped, such as most landing fields. The port used by landplanes should also be distinguished from the port used by seaplanes. The nature of the possible difficulties in the operation of all these ports is much the same, the difference between them being in the probable number of such difficulties and the expense in coping with them.

Obstacles — Liability to Suit. The operation of an airport may in many ways be an annoyance to abutting and neighboring landowners. These annoyances may be divided into those which can be obviated by the conduct of the field in accordance with good modern practice, and annoyances which cannot be so avoided and therefore may be said to be, for the present at least, inherent in the business. Unnecessary annoyance, such as dust which can be kept down, undue noise, etc., may be sufficient to be a nuisance which the landowner incommoded may prevent by injunction or for which he may recover damages as a nuisance. The protection of the airport from action for unnecessary annoyance is the conduct of the field in accordance with good modern practice, and calls for no further comment.

Freedom from successful suit by those who own or occupy nearby land cannot always, however, be secured by the proper conduct of an activity. Some essential industries are more or less necessarily objectionable in their operation, and necessarily placed somewhere. The question is whether they are properly located. As placed such industries have in many cases been held by the courts to be a nuisance, and from the danger of such a holding the airport would not seem to be immune.

Physical Obstacles. To the aviator while in the upper air structures below him are not a menace. In landing, however, the flier approaches and leaves the airport at an angle of about seven to one. It is therefore structures in the neighborhood of the port which are most likely to be a peril to him.

These structures have been found to be buildings, especially tall buildings, towers on buildings or tower buildings, smokestacks, radio towers, flag poles and similar structures, telephone and telegraph lines, and especially high-tension electric lines. Tall trees may also be a serious obstacle. In general it has been found that the aviator needs protection from obstacles such as these in leaving and approaching an airport of reasonable size according to present standards, for a distance of about 1500 feet in all directions from the outer boundaries of the port.

In addition smoke and gases from industrial operations in the vicinity of the port may in many ways interfere with its operation.

Protection from Suit — Location by Law. An airport is sometimes specifically located by statute or by the license of a body acting by state authority.[1] This would seem to be a legal determination that the location of the port was, all things considered, proper. Zoning regulations sometimes admit an airport unconditionally into any zoning district. This would seem to establish its suitability to the district but not its location at a given spot in the district. Under most of the zoning ordinances at present in force in this country an airport is admitted to any zoning district, but only on application to a board of zoning appeals, which may in this case, as always, impose conditions. This may well be held to be full proof of the propriety of the exact location of the port and a bar to suit. (76)

Protection from Obstacles — Zoning. The best protection of an airport from uses disadvantageous to it on neighboring land is the exclusion of such uses from its neighborhood. This may measurably be accomplished by zoning. By this means the general height of future structures in the district may be kept down and the erection of tall office buildings and factories with their smokestacks, smoke, and gases forbidden.

There can be no valid zoning regulation especially in the interest of the port; it can be considered only in connection with all the other interests and appropriate uses of land in the neighborhood and a proper regulation made for the district as a whole. In a locality where the price of land is moderate, the existing buildings few and low, and the district suited to residential development, a residential zone may be created embracing the airport and an area around it, in so far as of similar character, with a low height limit throughout it. In such a district, in all proba-

[1] See p. 122 above.

bility, there would be no existing tall business buildings and no factories with tall chimneys giving out smoke and fumes. In neighborhoods, however, in which higher residential structures or business or industrial buildings are the appropriate use of the land, zoning must accord with this character of the land, and the laying out of an airport will not sufficiently change that character to make any other regulation reasonable and therefore valid.

Manifestly any zoning limitation of the height of all structures in the district a given distance from its outer boundaries at an angle of seven or ten to one is impossible (77); for it is a serious burden on neighboring land in the special interest of the port and does not in any proper sense treat all similar land in the district in the same way. It would seem reasonable, however, in a residential district containing an airport, to forbid exceptional and non-essential structures like towers and flag poles, rising above the general height limit of the district, in spite of the fact that such structures are usually permitted in these districts; for the airport is a use of a large tract in the district and may rightfully be given its due share of consideration in framing the restrictions for the district. And if these taller non-essentials may be forbidden completely, it seems obvious that they may be prohibited only in so far as they exceed the general height limit beyond an angle of seven to one or ten to one for a reasonable distance in all directions from the outer boundaries of the port.

The regulation of the height of non-essential structures at a seven or ten to one angle seems clearly to be zoning; if it could not be supported on the legal principles upon which zoning is founded, it is difficult to see how it could be supported at all. No addition to the usual zoning enabling act or special legislation of any sort is needed to enable local governments, having the power to zone, to make this regulation wherever proper; indeed, it seems impossible to frame any legislation more appropriate to that end or so readily defended in the courts. Nor would it be helpful to suggest the phraseology of a clause to be inserted in local zoning ordinances for the purpose, since they must vary to suit local circumstances and situations.

There would seem to be no reason why the port of a semi-public corporation or public utility, engaged in state or interstate commerce, as well as the port publicly owned and operated, should not be considered in the zoning of the district in which it is situated; and even a private port. Obviously, however, much more consideration in so doing would be given to the public port. In the same way ports used wholly or partly for auxiliary purposes, such as manufacture or storage of planes, especially if operated by an aviation company engaged in commerce, should be given appropriate attention.

Protection by Utility Regulation. The structures, wires, etc., of the industries at present regulated by public utility commissions are sometimes subject to local zoning ordinances, sometimes to a greater or less extent privileged by them or exempted from their operation. In so far as they are not regulated by zoning it would seem that they may best be controlled in the interest of aviation in so far as proper by the regulations of these commissions. (78) Such regulations may apply not only to future but to existing structures, appliances, and facilities, ordering their removal or relocation or the adoption of protective devices to prevent injury from them. Regulations of this sort are in exercise of the police power, for which no compensation is necessary. This is not unfair to the utilities since they are so regulated as to allow them to obtain from the public a fair net return for their services.

Protection of Seaplane Ports under Power over Commerce. What has been said above applies more or less to land under navigable water. It is possible to regulate it, however, in other ways. A seaplane while in the water is in some respects regarded as a vessel (79) and the United States, the states, and the local governments within the states, in so far as these local governments have been given power by the states to do so, may pass regulations in the interest of water navigation for the benefit of such a plane. Under this power obstacles to water navigation may be removed. The airport used by seaplanes, also, as an owner of riparian land, would have the right of water access from navigable water to the airport.

Protection by Eminent Domain. Zoning regulation is an exercise of the police power. Police power regulations may always be changed; for the police power cannot be lessened or abridged, but always remains in full in the public for its protection. The airport, therefore, must submit to zoning changes to its disadvantage in the district in which it is situated, if such occur; and amendments of zoning ordinances increasing the height and bulk of buildings and changing the use of land from residential to business or industry are frequent in this country. The only power, therefore, which the aviator has of preventing such changes to his disadvantage is his influence, in common with other interests, over the public officials and voters of the community. If he desires any more permanent protection, he must resort to eminent domain with compensation. Laws giving municipalities the power to protect their airports by this means from increasing heights are already on our statute books. (80) They give the airport the right by eminent domain to demolish tall structures on neighboring land, to take the air rights over it, or to take the entire title to it excepting the right to use it for purposes not interfering with air navigation, regranting the landowner that right. There is no legal reason why the same rights should not be given aviation companies engaged in interstate and state commerce, as similar rights have in the past been given to other public utilities. There is as yet, however, no case in which this has been done. It should be noted that taking the entire title to a given piece of land when only the air rights in it are needed is not excess condemnation but a permissible method of acquiring rights to be used for the public purpose in question. In such cases rights thus acquired, when not needed or no longer needed, may be sold. This occurs often in the construction of subways and has been sustained by the courts. (81)

Such a taking, therefore, not being excess condemnation, does not require a state constitutional amendment as the basis of a statute authorizing it and is not dependent upon the validity of excess condemnation, which cannot as yet be said to be completely established.

Protection by Marking. In cases where it is impracticable on account of expense or for any other reason to prevent or relocate erections which by reason of height or for any other reason are a peril to the aviator in the use of the airport, it may be desirable to mark them. The marking to be effective should be placed completely around the exterior of the structure at one-third and two-thirds its height and at its top. It should consist of red lights at night and bands of yellow and black for daytime protection. The burden of marking the dangerous structure and maintaining the marking would be a heavy one, neither broadly nor evenly divided among the members of the community. It would therefore be unreasonable to impose this burden upon the owner of the structure under the police power without compensation. Like any other public utility, however, the airport may be given the right to place and maintain this easement useful to it in its business by eminent domain.

Trees. As already stated, tall trees near an airport, especially if opposite the end of the runway, may be a serious obstacle to the operation of a port. It is doubtful whether they could be controlled by zoning; for the burden of watching and limiting them would in many cases be too great.   They could of course be limited in height by eminent domain.

Spite Erections and Planting.   If trees are planted, fences or any structures erected, not for the legitimate use of the landowner but to impede the use of the airport, there is no need of resort to the ordinary principles of the police power or to eminent domain ; for they would be in some jurisdictions unlawful and may be made so by statute anywhere.   A precedent for such legislation is provided by statutes with regard to so-called "spite fences."   (82)

It might be claimed that the landowner erected the fence not in spite or to obtain compensation or force the purchase of his land or rights to it, but to prevent aviators from annoying him by low flight.   If such flight were within legal limits, such erection would clearly be illegal in jurisdictions forbidding spite erections.   If the flight apprehended was an illegal one, the structure would seem to be justified in law ; and without the structure the landowner would have the right to prevent such flight, or recover damages, by legal action.

PROTECTION OF NEIGHBORING PROPERTY

The nature, methods, and extent of the protection which the law affords to owners of property from annoyance by an airport in their neighborhood is apparent from what has already been said.   Abutting property owners have certain rights in the air space immediately above their land which they may vindicate by action ; all property owners in the neighborhood may appeal to the state or to the local zoning authorities for a due consideration of their interests if they deem it unfair that a port should be located near them ; for the legitimate conduct of the port, if sufficiently annoying, they may have a measure of redress more or less in accordance with the definiteness with which the exact site is determined ; and the illegitimate conduct of it they may, if sufficiently damaged, prevent by injunction or obtain compensation for by action for nuisance.

ADMINISTRATION

The general right of local governments to set up administration machinery and change it varies in different jurisdictions.   In so-called "home rule" municipalities this power is often extensive ; in other local governments, less.   There are a few statutes with relation to this power with regard to airports.

There is the same variation of ruling in different jurisdictions with regard to the right in general of municipalities empowered to engage in a given enterprise to lease it to others for operation. It has been held that a municipality cannot, in the absence of a statute authorizing it, so lease an airport. (83) There are now many statutes specifically granting this power. (84)

APPENDICES

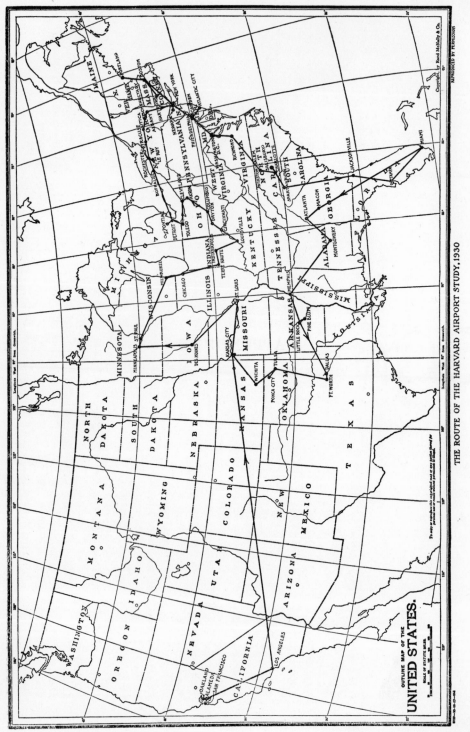

THE ROUTE OF THE HARVARD AIRPORT STUDY, 1930

OUTLINE MAP OF THE

UNITED STATES.

SCALE OF STATUTE MILES

134

APPENDIX 1

LIST OF AIRPORTS VISITED

With Information as to Ownership and Operation

City and State	Name of Airport	Owned By	Operated By
AKRON, O.	Akron Airport	City of Akron	City of Akron
ALAMEDA, CALIF.	Alameda Airport	City of Alameda	Alameda Airport, Inc.
ALBANY, N. Y.	Albany Airport	City of Albany	City of Albany
ARLINGTON, VA.	Hoover Field (serves Washington, D. C.)	International Airways, Inc.	Potomac Flying Service
ARLINGTON, VA.	Washington Airport (serves Washington, D. C.)	Washington Air Terminal, Inc.	Washington Flying Company
ATCHISON, KAN.	Atchison Airport	Fairfax Airports, Inc.	Fairfax Airports, Inc.
ATLANTA, GA.	Candler Field	City of Atlanta	City of Atlanta
ATLANTIC CITY, N. J.	Atlantic City Airport	Atlantic City	Atlantic City
BOSTON, MASS.	Boston Airport	Commonwealth of Massachusetts	City of Boston
BUFFALO, N. Y.	Buffalo Airport	City of Buffalo	City of Buffalo
CAMDEN, N. J.	Central Airport	Central Airport, Inc.	Central Airport, Inc.
CHARLOTTE, N. C.	Charlotte Airport	Charlotte Airport, Inc.	Charlotte Airport, Inc.
CHICAGO, ILL.	Chicago Airport	Chicago Board of Education	City of Chicago
CINCINNATI, O.	Lunken Airport	City of Cincinnati	City of Cincinnati
CLEVELAND, O.	Cleveland Airport	City of Cleveland	City of Cleveland
CLEVELAND, O.	Curtiss-Herrick Airport	Curtiss-Wright Airports Corporation	Curtiss-Wright Flying Service
COLUMBUS, O.	Port Columbus	City of Columbus	City of Columbus
DALLAS, TEX.	Curtiss-Wright Airport	Curtiss Flying Service	Curtiss-Wright Flying Service
DALLAS, TEX.	Hensley Field	City of Dallas	City of Dallas and U. S. Army
DALLAS, TEX.	Love Field	City of Dallas	City of Dallas
DAYTON, O.	Dayton Airport, Inc.	Dayton Airport, Inc.	Johnson Flying Service, Inc.

135

LIST OF AIRPORTS VISITED (*Continued*)

City and State	Name of Airport	Owned By	Operated By
DEARBORN, MICH.	Ford Airport	Ford Motor Company	Ford Motor Company
DES MOINES, IA.	Des Moines Airport	Private Owner	City of Des Moines
DETROIT, MICH.	Detroit City Airport	City of Detroit	City of Detroit
EAST ST. LOUIS, ILL.	Curtiss-Steinberg Field	St. Louis Air Terminals, Inc.	St. Louis Air Terminals, Inc.
FORT WORTH, TEX.	Meacham Field	City of Fort Worth	City of Fort Worth
GARDEN CITY, N. Y.	Roosevelt Field (serves New York City)	Roosevelt Field, Inc.	Roosevelt Field, Inc.
GLENDALE, CALIF.	Grand Central Air Terminal	Curtiss-Wright Airports Corporation	Grand Central Air Terminal, Inc.
GLENVIEW, ILL.	Curtiss-Reynolds Field (serves Chicago, Ill.)	Chicago Air Terminal, Inc.	Curtiss-Wright Flying Service
GROSSE ILE, MICH.	Grosse Ile Airport (serves Detroit, Mich.)	Detroit Aircraft Corporation	Grosse Ile Airport Corporation
HARTFORD, CONN.	Brainard Field	City of Hartford	City of Hartford
INDIANAPOLIS, IND.	Capitol Airways Airport	Private Owner	Capitol Airways, Inc.
INDIANAPOLIS, IND.	Hoosier Airport	Private Owner	Hoosier Airport Corporation
INDIANAPOLIS, IND.	Indianapolis Airport	City of Indianapolis	City of Indianapolis
INDIANAPOLIS, IND.	Stout Field	State of Indiana	Armory Board of the State of Indiana and Curtiss-Wright Flying Service
JACKSONVILLE, FLA.	Jacksonville Airport	City of Jacksonville	City of Jacksonville
KANSAS CITY, KAN.	Fairfax Airport	Fairfax Airports, Inc.	Fairfax Airports, Inc.
KANSAS CITY, MO.	Kansas City Airport	Kansas City, Mo.	Kansas City, Mo.
LE ROY, N. Y.	Donald Woodward Airport	Private Owner	Donald Woodward Flying Service, Inc.
LOS ANGELES, CALIF.	Metropolitan Airport	Los Angeles Metropolitan Airport, Inc.	Los Angeles Metropolitan Airport, Inc.
LOS ANGELES, CALIF.	Mines Field	Private Owner	City of Los Angeles
LOS ANGELES, CALIF.	Western Air Express Terminal	Western Air Express	Western Air Express

Louisville, Ky.	Bowman Field	Board of Park Commissioners of City of Louisville	Louisville and Jefferson County Air Board
Macon, Ga.	Miller Airport	City of Macon	Georgia Flying Service
Memphis, Tenn.	Memphis Airport	Private Owner	City of Memphis
Miami, Fla.	Miami Airport	City of Miami	City of Miami
Miami, Fla.	Miami Dirigible Airport	City of Miami	Goodyear Zeppelin Corporation
Miami, Fla.	Miami Seaplane Base	Venetian Island Corporation	City of Miami
Miami, Fla.	Pan-American Airport	Pan-American Airways	Pan-American Airways
Milwaukee, Wis.	Curtiss-Milwaukee Airport	Milwaukee Air Terminals, Inc.	Curtiss-Wright Flying Service
Milwaukee, Wis.	Maitland Field	City of Milwaukee	City of Milwaukee
Milwaukee County, Wis.	Milwaukee County Airport	County of Milwaukee	County of Milwaukee
Minneapolis, Minn.	Minneapolis Airport	Minneapolis Park Board	Minneapolis Park Board
Montgomery, Ala.	Montgomery Airport	City of Montgomery	City of Montgomery
Newark, N. J.	Newark Airport	City of Newark	City of Newark
Oakland, Calif.	Oakland Airport	City of Oakland	City of Oakland
Orange, Mass.	Orange-Athol Airport	Orange-Athol Airport Corporation	Orange-Athol Airport Corporation
Parkville, Mo.	Parkville Airport	Fairfax Airports, Inc.	Fairfax Airports, Inc.
Philadelphia, Pa.	Philadelphia Airport	City of Philadelphia	Ludington Philadelphia Flying Service
Pine Bluff, Ark.	Toney Field	Arkansas Airport Company	Arkansas Airport Company
Ponca City, Okla.	Everett Taylor Airport	Private Owner	Ponca City and the Continental Oil Company
Ponca City, Okla.	Ponca City Airport	State of Oklahoma	Ponca City and the Continental Oil Company
Pontiac, Mich.	Pontiac Airport	City of Pontiac	City of Pontiac
Portland, Me.	Portland Airport	Portland Airport Corporation	Curtiss-Wright Flying Service
Richmond, Va.	Richard E. Byrd Airport	City of Richmond	Pitcairn Aviation Corporation
Rochester, N. Y.	Rochester Airport	City of Rochester	City of Rochester
St. Joseph, Mo.	Rosecrans Field	City of St. Joseph	Fairfax Airports, Inc.
St. Louis, Mo.	St. Louis Airport	City of St. Louis	City of St. Louis
St. Paul, Minn.	St. Paul Airport	City of St. Paul	City of St. Paul

LIST OF AIRPORTS VISITED (*Continued*)

City and State	Name of Airport	Owned By	Operated By
SALISBURY, N. C.	Salisbury Airport	City of Salisbury	City of Salisbury
SAN FRANCISCO, CALIF.	Mills Field	Private Owner	City of San Francisco
SCHENECTADY, N. Y.	Schenectady Airport	Schenectady Airport, Inc.	Schenectady Airport, Inc.
SPARTANBURG, S. C.	Spartanburg Airport	City of Spartanburg	Pitcairn Aviation Corporation
SYRACUSE, N. Y.	Syracuse Airport	City of Syracuse	City of Syracuse
TAMPA, FLA.	Drew Field	Private Owner	City of Tampa
TERRE HAUTE, IND.	Dresser Field	City of Terre Haute	City of Terre Haute
TOLEDO, O.	Toledo Airport	Private Owner	City of Toledo
TOLEDO, O.	Transcontinental Airport	Transcontinental Airport, Inc.	Transcontinental Airport, Inc.
TULSA, OKLA.	Tulsa Airport	Held in trust by the Exchange Trust Company	Board of Underwriters
UTICA, N. Y.	Utica Airport	City of Utica	City of Utica
VALLEY STREAM, N. Y.	Curtiss-Valley Stream Field	Curtiss-Valley Stream Field, Inc.	Curtiss-Valley Stream Field, Inc.
WAYNE COUNTY, MICH.	Wayne County Airport	Wayne County	Wayne County
WESTON, MO.	Weston Field	Fairfax Airports, Inc.	Fairfax Airports, Inc.
WICHITA, KAN.	Wichita Municipal Airport	City of Wichita	City of Wichita
WINSTON-SALEM, N. C.	Winston-Salem Airport	Winston-Salem Foundation	Miller Municipal Airport Commission

138

APPENDIX 2

POPULATION OF CITIES VISITED

AKRON	240,000 [2]	MEMPHIS	190,200 [1]
ALAMEDA	31,876 [3]	MIAMI	156,700 [1]
ALBANY	120,400 [1]	MILWAUKEE	544,200 [1]
ARLINGTON	1,863 [8]	MINNEAPOLIS	455,900 [1]
ATCHISON	25,455 [4]	MONTGOMERY	63,100 [1]
ATLANTA	255,100 [1]	NEWARK	473,600 [1]
ATLANTIC CITY	54,700 [1]	OAKLAND	274,100 [1]
BOSTON	799,200 [1]	ORANGE	5,141 [5]
BUFFALO	555,800 [1]	PARKVILLE	619 [7]
CAMDEN	135,400 [1]	PHILADELPHIA	2,064,200 [1]
CHARLOTTE	82,100 [1]	PINE BLUFF	21,611 [2]
CHICAGO	3,157,400 [1]	PONCA CITY	17,000 [6]
CINCINNATI	413,700 [1]	PONTIAC	61,500 [1]
CLEVELAND	1,010,300 [1]	PORTLAND	78,600 [1]
COLUMBUS	299,000 [1]	RICHMOND	194,400 [1]
DALLAS	217,800 [7]	ROCHESTER	328,200 [1]
DAYTON	184,500 [1]	ST. JOSEPH	78,500 [1]
DEARBORN	2,470 [1]	ST. LOUIS	848,100 [1]
DES MOINES	151,900 [1]	ST. PAUL	358,162 [2]
DETROIT	1,378,900 [1]	SALISBURY	13,884 [7]
EAST ST. LOUIS	74,000 [1]	SAN FRANCISCO	585,300 [1]
FORT WORTH	170,600 [1]	SCHENECTADY	93,300 [1]
GARDEN CITY	3,141 [3]	SPARTANBURG	22,638 [7]
GLENDALE	21,290 [3]	SYRACUSE	199,300 [1]
GLENVIEW	760 [7]	TAMPA	113,400 [1]
HARTFORD	172,300 [1]	TERRE HAUTE	73,500 [1]
INDIANAPOLIS	382,100 [1]	TOLEDO	313,200 [1]
JACKSONVILLE	140,700 [1]	TULSA	170,500 [1]
KANSAS CITY, KAN.	118,300 [1]	UTICA	104,200 [1]
KANSAS CITY, MO.	391,000 [1]	VALLEY STREAM	7,313 [4]
LE ROY	4,348 [4]	WESTON	991 [7]
LOS ANGELES	1,420,000 [2]	WICHITA	99,300 [1]
LOUISVILLE	329,400 [1]	WINSTON-SALEM	80,000 [1]
MACON	61,200 [1]		

[1] Figures from U. S. Dept. of Commerce, population estimate as of July 1, 1928, of municipalities having 30,000 or more inhabitants on Jan. 1, 1920.

[2] Figures from 1930 World Almanac, Estimated Population of Big U. S. Cities, July 1, 1928.

[3] 1925 population. Figures from Chamber of Commerce of the U. S., Supplement to City Planning and Zoning Accomplishments — a report compiled by the Civic Development Department.

[4] 1925 State Census. World Almanac 1930.

[5] 1925 Decennial Census of Commonwealth of Massachusetts.

[6] 1927 Local Census. (See "Our Cities To-day and To-morrow," p. 306.)

[7] 1920 Federal Census.

[8] Figures from estimated population of 1920, Rand McNally Commercial Atlas (1928).

APPENDIX 3

PERSONS WHO FURNISHED MAJOR INFORMATION FOR
THE AIRPORT STUDY

The authors regret that limits of space prevent the listing of all officials and citizens in the many cities visited who kindly gave a brief interview to the field representative during the airport study.

ADAMS, D. G., Spartanburg, S. C.
ALLEN, FRANK R., Pine Bluff, Ark.
AMBROSE, FRANK J., Valley Stream, N. Y.

BAGGETT, FREDERICK R., Albany, N. Y.
BAKER, HAROLD W., Rochester, N. Y.
BALDWIN, H. BEVAN, Atlantic City, N. J.
BEACH, E. J., Buffalo, N. Y.
BELL, A. T., Atlantic City, N. J.
BELL, J. HASLETT, Des Moines, Ia.
BENNETT, E. O., Ponca City, Okla.
BENNETT, H. C., New York, N. Y.
BERRY, MAJOR JOHN, Cleveland, O.
BERTHE, A. E., Minneapolis, Minn.
BLACK, ARCHIBALD, New York, N. Y.
BLEE, COLONEL HARRY H., Washington, D. C.
BLUCHER, WALTER H., Detroit, Mich.
BOWERS, G. M., Richmond, Va.
BOYER, FRANK M., Terre Haute, Ind.
BRANDT, WILLIAM, Toledo, O.
BROOKS, H. C., Indianapolis, Ind.
BROWN, MAYOR BEN HILL, Spartanburg, S. C.
BUSH, HOLLIS, Miami, Fla.
BUTTON, SCOTT, Schenectady, N. Y.

CANADA, COLONEL J. W., Memphis, Tenn.
CANNON, FRANK F., Buffalo, N. Y.
CAPES, WILLIAM P., Albany, N. Y.
CAREY, WILLIAM N., St. Paul, Minn.
CARLTON, D. W., Fort Worth, Tex.
CARR, O. E., Fort Worth, Tex.
CASEY, J. A., Chicago, Ill.

CAVANAUGH, W. F., Milwaukee, Wis.
CENTNER, MAJOR WILLIAM F., Columbus, O.
CLARK, JAMES C., Jacksonville, Fla.
COATH, CAPTAIN ROBERT, Portland, Me.
COAN, MAYOR GEORGE W., JR., Winston-Salem, N. C.
CONLEY, CHARLES E., Cleveland, O.
CONNELL, WILLIAM H., Philadelphia, Pa.
COOK, H. WEIR, Indianapolis, Ind.
COOPER, J. H., St. Paul, Minn.
COSGROVE, T. F., Milwaukee, Wis.
COX, MAJOR CHARLES E., JR., Indianapolis, Ind.
COX, PAUL S., Terre Haute, Ind.
COYNER, STRATTON, Mineola, N. Y.
CRAIG, R. F., Kansas City, Mo.
CULBERTSON, WALLACE D., Miami, Fla.

DAVIS, R. WALLACE, Tampa, Fla.
DOE, W. W., Montgomery, Ala.
DOLAN, C. H., Richmond, Va.
DUFFY, N. E., Buffalo, N. Y.
DUNCAN, L. H., Spartanburg, S. C.

ECKERT, MAJOR SAMUEL B., Philadelphia, Pa.
EDSON, CAPTAIN ALBERT L., Boston, Mass.
EMBRY, T. HIGBEE, Cincinnati, O.

FARRELL, ROY C., Kansas City, Mo.
FISHER, CHARLES F., Akron, O.
FITCH, HARRY E., JR., Terre Haute, Ind.
FITZGERALD, JOSEPH F., JR., Albany, N. Y.
FOULKES, ARTHUR F., Terre Haute, Ind.

FRANZHEIM, KENNETH, New York, N. Y.
FREELAND, B. B., Miami, Fla.
FREEMAN, HARRY J., New York, N. Y.
FRITSCHE, GEORGE W., Grosse Ile, Mich.
FULLER, WILLIAM G., Fort Worth, Tex.
FULTON, B. E., Akron, O.

GARBER, J. OTIS, St. Louis, Mo.
GENG, F. J., St. Paul, Minn.
GOLDSBOROUGH, PAUL, St. Louis, Mo.
GREEN, W. SANGER, Camden, N. J.
GRIFFITH, E. C., Charlotte, N. C.

HALE, ROBERT L., New York, N. Y.
HAMMOND, L. D., Minneapolis, Minn.
HANNAM, E. B., Syracuse, N. Y.
HARDIN, C. L., Chicago, Ill.
HARE, S. HERBERT, Kansas City, Mo.
HARTSFIELD, WILLIAM B., Atlanta, Ga.
HAYMAN, MORTON F., Terre Haute, Ind.
HEARIN, JESSE B., Montgomery, Ala.
HEATH, REGINALD I., Utica, N. Y.
HEERMANCE, A. H., Miami, Fla.
HERLIHY, ELISABETH M., Boston, Mass.
HERROLD, GEORGE H., St. Paul, Minn.
HILL, PARKER, Cleveland, O.
HILL, PERLEY J., Philadelphia, Pa.
HOELSCHER, L. W., Fort Worth, Tex.
HOLLAND, PAUL, Detroit, Mich.
HOLMAN, C. W., St. Paul, Minn.
HORN, A. J., Toledo, O.
HORNER, W. W., St. Louis, Mo.
HORTON, R. HARLAND, Philadelphia, Pa.
HOWARD, E. A., Milwaukee, Wis.
HOWARD, CLARENCE E., Syracuse, N. Y.
HUGHES, FRANK, Columbus, O.

JOHNSON, FRED W., Philadelphia, Pa.
JORDAN, R. G., Macon, Ga.

KAISER, FRANK A., Milwaukee, Wis.
KENNEDY, G. D., Pontiac, Mich.
KINCAID, R. L., Syracuse, N. Y.
KINGERY, ROBERT, Chicago, Ill.
KINTZ, ELMER McD., Washington, D. C.
KISER, DANIEL, Milwaukee, Wis.
KLEWER, JUDGE EDWARD B., Memphis,
   Tenn.
KNOX, CLARENCE M., Hartford, Conn.
KUESTER, C. O., Charlotte, N. C.

LAIRD, MAJOR ROLAND A., Dallas, Tex.
LAMBERT, A. B., St. Louis, Mo.
LANDIS, REED G., Chicago, Ill.
LAWRENCE, F. E., JR., St. Louis, Mo.
LAYFIELD, E. R., Macon, Ga.
LEDERER, JEROME, New York, N. Y.
LEE, A. W., Louisville, Ky.
LENNON, JAMES J., Albany, N. Y.
LEWIS, JOHN V., Rochester, N. Y.
LOTHROP, ERNEST E., Orange, Mass.

MACDONALD, ALFRED, Wichita, Kan.
MARSHALL, R. C., Cleveland, O.
MASON, L. G., Montgomery, Ala.
McCRARY, DEWITT, Macon, Ga.
McKERNAN, C. A., Utica, N. Y.
MEISTER, LOUIS, Cleveland, O.
MELVILLE, GEORGE W., Cincinnati, O.
MILLER, EDWIN A., Rochester, N. Y.
MOORE, PAUL H., Indianapolis, Ind.
MOOT, RICHMOND D., Schenectady, N. Y.
MULOCK, MAYOR E. H., Des Moines, Ia.
MUNRO, W. B., Cambridge, Mass.
MURPHY, J. C., Louisville, Ky.

NASSR, A. M., Toledo, O.
NICHOLSON, BROWN, Macon, Ga.
NORTON, JOHN K., Detroit, Mich.

ODELL, L. L., Miami, Fla.
OLIN, ROBERT N., Cincinnati, O.
ORMISTON, T. N., Kansas City, Mo.
O'RYAN, GENERAL JOHN F., New York,
   N. Y.
O'TOOLE, PETER J., JR., Newark, N. J.
OVERTON, MAYOR WATKINS, Memphis,
   Tenn.

PARKER, GEORGE O., Macon, Ga.
PARKS, O. R., Robertson, Mo.
PAUL, CHARLES H., Dayton, O.
PIASECKI, MAJOR STANLEY, Milwaukee,
   Wis.
PIETY, CHARLES E., Terre Haute, Ind.
POLLET, BENJAMIN A., New York, N. Y.
PUTNAM, CHARLTON D., Dayton, O.

RABBITT, P. J., Washington, D. C.
REEL, RUSSELL, Des Moines, Ia.
REINHARDT, R. R., Kansas City, Mo.

REX, FREDERICK, Chicago, Ill.
RICE, MAXWELL JAY, Miami, Fla.
RICKARD, V. A., Schenectady, N. Y.
RIDDLE, JOHN PAUL, Cincinnati, O.
RITTER, WILLIAM T., Winston-Salem, N. C.
ROBERTS, C. F., Glenview, Ill.
ROBERTSON, JOHN P., Flushing, N. Y.
ROBINSON, MAYOR PAT L., Little Rock, Ark.
ROGERS, MAJOR H. W., Louisville, Ky.
ROHLAND, O. W., JR., St. Paul, Minn.

SALISBURY, H. L., St. Louis, Mo.
SALTUS, R. S., JR., Camden, N. J.
SATTERFIELD, JOHN M., Buffalo, N. Y.
SHANK, ROBERT F., Indianapolis, Ind.
SHAW, B. RUSSELL, St. Louis, Mo.
SHORT, C. W., JR., Tulsa, Okla.
SIMONS, GEORGE W., JR., Jacksonville, Fla.
SMART, HERBERT, Macon, Ga.
SNEED, PRESTON, Dallas, Tex.

TALIAFERRO, A. PENDLETON, JR., Washington, D. C.

TAYLOR, HOLLINSHEAD N., Philadelphia, Pa.
TIPPEE, J. M., Des Moines, Ia.
TORRAS, R. W., Atlanta, Ga.
TULLY, MAJOR J. K., St. Louis, Mo.

VAN BUREN, S. G., Toledo, O.
VEDDER, A. L., Rochester, N. Y.
VERNON, VICTOR, New York, N. Y.

WALKER, WATSON, Macon, Ga.
WALLACE, W. J., Detroit, Mich.
WALTON, KENNETH B., Atlantic City, N. J.
WATERS, R. V., Miami, Fla.
WEBB, J. GRISWOLD, Albany, N. Y.
WILLIAMS, EDWIN M., Memphis, Tenn.
WIRTH, THEODORE, Minneapolis, Minn.
WOOD, MAJOR E. A., Dallas, Tex.
WRIGHT, A. J., Columbus, O.
WRIGHT, WALTER, Chicago, Ill.
WUNDER, ALBERT B., Cincinnati, O.
WYMAN, PHELPS, Milwaukee, Wis.
WYNNE, JOHN S., South Washington, Va.

YONGE, J. E., Miami, Fla.
YOUNG, W. C., Akron, O.

APPENDIX 4

AIRPORT MANAGERS' SUGGESTIONS AND CRITICISMS AS TO CONDITIONS AT THEIR AIRPORTS

(*A*) In answering the question "What suggestions or criticism have you to offer as to conditions at your airport?", the management at thirty-eight municipal airports gave the following answers:

    16 wanted more land.   Average acreage of these airports is 289.

    8 wanted more money.

    7 wanted a location closer to the heart of the city.   Average distance of these airports from the post office is 7 miles.

    5 wanted the flying field brought to a better grade.

    4 wanted better highways.

    3 wanted school activity segregated.

    3 wanted a better surface for the flying field.

    3 wanted better lighting equipment.

    3 wanted more of the land developed for flying purposes.   Average amount of land developed at these airports for these purposes is 24 acres.

    2 wanted more operation facilities.

    2 wanted less political interference.

    2 wanted less hazardous surroundings.

    2 wanted the airport protected by a zoning ordinance.

    1 wanted the flying field more thoroughly drained.

    1 wanted better fire protection.

    1 wanted better water connections.

    1 wanted the area occupied by the airport annexed by the city.

    1 wanted the dust nuisance reduced.

    1 wanted better traffic control.

    1 wanted the smoke nuisance reduced.

    1 wanted an administration building.

    8 were completely satisfied.   Average size of these airports is 586 acres, average developed area 315 acres, average distance from post office is 9 miles.

(*B*) The management at fourteen commercial airports gave the following answers:

    1 wanted more land.   Acreage of this airport is 150.

    5 wanted a location closer to the heart of the city.   Average distance of these airports from the post office is 12 miles.

    1 wanted better lighting equipment.

    2 wanted less hazardous surroundings.

    1 wanted better hangar facilities.

    6 were completely satisfied.   Average size of these airports is 270 acres, average developed area 240.5 acres, average distance from the post office is 8 miles.

APPENDIX 5

AGENCIES REPORTED AS CONCERNED IN THE SELECTION OF AIRPORT SITES

Aeronautics Branch of the Department of Commerce . . . . 4 [1]
American Legion 1
Army and Navy Officials 9
Aviation Commission (City or State) 8
Bureau of Budget and Efficiency 1
Chamber of Commerce 9
Citizens' Committee 9
City Council 5
City and Regional Planning Commissions 2
Consulting Engineer 1
County Surveyor 1
Department of Water and Power 1
Mayor 4
National Aeronautical Association 4
Park Department 3
Pilots 17
Private Concern Building the Airport or Operating from It 25
Public Utility Company 1
Public Works Department 3

[1] Figures indicate the number of airports reporting the agency as having been concerned in the site selection.

APPENDIX 6

FACTORS WHICH WERE REPORTED AS DETERMINING THE SELECTION OF AIRPORT SITES

Cost of Drainage, low . . . . 14 [1]
Cost of Grading, low 12
Cost of Improvements, low 7
Cost of Land, low 23
Ease of Acquisition of Land in Large Parcels 9
Elevation, high 6
Expansion, opportunity for 2
Highway, well located in relation to 24
Land Already Owned 6
Land and Water Both Available for Landing Purposes 4
Obstructions, freedom from 19
Only Satisfactory Site Available 7
Park Adjacent to Airport 1
Political Pressure 2
Proximity to Centers of Population 33
Public Utilities Readily Available 4
Railroad Adjacent or Near 9
Smoke and Fog, freedom from 10
Soil, fertile 4
Transportation Readily Available 9
Used as Landing Field Previously 4
Unnecessary to Fly Over City on Main Airway Routes 2
Windward of Town, location to 2

[1] Figures indicate the number of airports reporting each item as one of the principal factors.

APPENDIX 7

NUMBER OF PEOPLE WHO COME TO THE AIRPORT

Name	Average Number of People on an Ordinary Day in Summer	Number of People on a Week-end in Summer	Largest Number of People on any one Day
Akron [1]	1500 [2]		45,000
Albany	500–600	3000–7000	10,000
Arlington			
Hoover Field	200	2000	
Washington Airport . . .	400–500	1000–1200	1500–2000
Atchison		2000 [2]	
Atlanta	500	6000 [2]	50,000
Atlantic City	500	2000	3000–4000
Boston	500–1000		10,000
Buffalo	400–500	15,000 [2]	75,000
Camden	500	2000–5000	25,000
Charlotte			10,000
Chicago	100	1000 [2]	200,000
Cincinnati	200	5000 [2]	35,000
Cleveland			
Cleveland Airport	3000–4000	28,000 [2]	140,000
Curtiss-Herrick Airport . .		200–300 [2]	
Columbus	2000–5000	10,000–15,000	50,000
Dallas			
Hensley Field		200	7000–8000
Love Field	1500–2500	15,000–25,000	80,000
Dayton	300	5000	15,000
Des Moines	100	2000	30,000
Detroit		10,000	75,000
Fort Worth	400–500	2000–3000	10,000
Garden City	1000	10,000	150,000
Glenview	150	5000 [2]	40,000–50,000
Grosse Ile		5000 [2]	12,000
Hartford		5000 [2]	75,000
Indianapolis			
Capitol Airways Airport . .	100	5000 [2]	10,000
Hoosier Airport	100	10,000–15,000 [2]	75,000
Jacksonville	100–500	10,000 [2]	30,000–40,000
Kansas City, Kan.	5000	10,000–30,000	259,221 [3]

[1] For the name of the airport in each case, see Appendix 1, List of Airports Visited.

[2] Sunday only.

[3] Estimate made on basis of 3 people per automobile.

146

NAME	AVERAGE NUMBER OF PEOPLE ON AN ORDINARY DAY IN SUMMER	NUMBER OF PEOPLE ON A WEEK-END IN SUMMER	LARGEST NUMBER OF PEOPLE ON ANY ONE DAY
KANSAS CITY, MO.		5000	20,000
LE ROY	100	20,000 [1]	86,000
LOUISVILLE	200	5000–10,000	20,000
MACON	100	1000	10,000
MEMPHIS	500	30,000	80,000
MIAMI			
Miami Airport	25–75	500–2000	20,000
Dirigible Airport		1000–5000	
Miami Seaplane Base . . .	100	500	
Miami Pan-American Airport			30,000
MILWAUKEE			
Maitland Field		300–500	10,000
Milwaukee County	100–200	10,000	12,000
MINNEAPOLIS	400–500	10,000 [1]	75,000
MONTGOMERY	10–100	4000 [1]	
NEWARK	2500–3500	5000–10,000	60,000
ORANGE	50–100	100–500	10,000
PHILADELPHIA	200	1000–10,000	10,000
PINE BLUFF	500	2500–3000 [1]	18,000
PONCA CITY			
Everett Taylor Airport . .		200–300	
PONTIAC	100	500–1000 [1]	50,000
PORTLAND, ME.		2000–3000	
RICHMOND		1000	2000–2500
ROCHESTER	100	300–5000	10,000
ST. JOSEPH			15,000
ST. PAUL	200	3000 [1]	75,000
SCHENECTADY	100–200	500–1000 [1]	10,000
SPARTANBURG		500	
SYRACUSE	200–500	5000 [1]	30,000
TAMPA	150	400 [1]	2000
TERRE HAUTE	500	5000 [1]	25,000
TOLEDO			
Toledo Airport		20,000	40,000
Transcontinental Airport . .	0–60	200–10,000 [1]	40,000
TULSA		5000	15,000
UTICA	500	3000–5000	27,000
VALLEY STREAM	100	8000	10,000
WICHITA	500	10,000 [1]	20,000
WINSTON-SALEM		1000–2000	10,000

[1] Sunday only.

APPENDIX 8

REPORTED DAILY ACTIVITY AT AIRPORTS VISITED

NAME	SCHEDULED MAIL PLANES	SCHEDULED TRANSPORT PLANES		AVERAGE TRANSIENT PLANES	AVERAGE CHARTERED TRIPS, SIGHT-SEEING, ETC.	AVERAGE SCHOOL PLANE HOPS	TOTAL ARRIVALS AND DEPARTURES REPORTED
		Arrivals	Departures				
AKRON [1]	3	²		5½			
ALAMEDA	8	6	7	1			
ALBANY		9	9				
ARLINGTON							
Hoover Field				3			
Washington Airport	5			3			
ATLANTA				2			
ATLANTIC CITY	3			1½			
BOSTON		8	8	20			30
BUFFALO		1	1	9			
CAMDEN				2			
CHICAGO	16	8	8	25	10	80	
CINCINNATI	8	8	8	1⅓			
CLEVELAND							
Cleveland Airport	11	24	24	32			
COLUMBUS	1	1	1	30	30	100	
DALLAS							
Love Field	3	6	6				60

[1] For the name of the airport in each case, see Appendix 1, List of Airports Visited.
[2] A blank does not necessarily mean a lack of activity. It may simply mean a failure to report it.

Dayton	2			5			
Detroit	3			16			
Fort Worth		6	6	5		16	100
Garden City				2			
Grosse Ile				1			
Hartford							
Indianapolis							
Capitol Airways Airport				3			
Hoosier Airport				1			
Stout Field				5			
Jacksonville		5	5	5	39	127	15
Kansas City, Kan.				12			
Kansas City, Mo.							
Le Roy				2			
Los Angeles							
Metropolitan Airport							
Mines Field				15			149
Louisville	2			2			
Macon	2			$\frac{2}{3}$			
Memphis				3			
Miami							
Miami Airport	1	1	1				
Pan-American Airport	10	10	10				72 a week in and out all scheduled
Milwaukee							
Milwaukee County Airport	6	4	4	$1\frac{1}{2}$	$2\frac{2}{3}$		
Minneapolis				2	16		
Montgomery							
Newark		4	5				
Oakland	2			2			
Philadelphia				4			
Pine Bluff							

REPORTED DAILY ACTIVITY AT AIRPORTS VISITED (*Continued*)

| NAME | SCHEDULED MAIL PLANES | SCHEDULED TRANSPORT PLANES | | AVERAGE TRANSIENT PLANES | AVERAGE CHARTERED TRIPS, SIGHT-SEEING, ETC. | AVERAGE SCHOOL PLANE HOPS | TOTAL ARRIV-ALS AND DE-PARTURES REPORTED |
		Arrivals	Departures				
PONCA CITY							
Everett Taylor Airport	1	1	1				
PONTIAC	2	2	2	1			
RICHMOND	2			1			
ROCHESTER	2						
ST. LOUIS							
St. Louis Airport	5	7	7	1			
ST. PAUL	2	3	3	3			
SAN FRANCISCO							6 a day
SCHENECTADY	2						
SPARTANBURG	2						
SYRACUSE	2						
TERRE HAUTE	2			5			
TOLEDO	10			5			
Transcontinental Airport	6	18	18				
TULSA	2			1			
UTICA	2	8	8	2			
WICHITA							
WINSTON-SALEM							

APPENDIX 9

SQUARE FEET OF TOTAL AND DEVELOPED AREAS OF AIRPORTS FOR WHICH THESE FIGURES WERE GIVEN

Number of Airports Reporting Both 50

NAME	TOTAL ACREAGE	DEVELOPED ACREAGE
AKRON [1]	900	80
ALBANY	235	235
ARLINGTON		
Hoover Field	38.5	38.5
ATLANTA	300	150
ATLANTIC CITY	112	112
BOSTON	131	131
BUFFALO	555	200
CAMDEN	150	150
CHARLOTTE	220	150
CHICAGO	320	160
CINCINNATI	1000	450
CLEVELAND		
Curtiss-Herrick Airport	277	160
Cleveland Airport	1085	700
DALLAS		
Love Field	173	173
DAYTON	310	310
DES MOINES	160	160
DETROIT	250	250
FORT WORTH	425	213
GLENVIEW	510	380
HARTFORD	425	125
INDIANAPOLIS		
Capitol Airways Airport	176	90
Hoosier Airport	80	80
JACKSONVILLE	175	75
KANSAS CITY, KAN.	779	244
KANSAS CITY, MO.	687	400
LE ROY	150	150
LOS ANGELES		
Western Air Express Terminal	500	380

[1] For the name of the airport in each case, see Appendix 1, List of Airports Visited.

SQUARE FEET OF TOTAL AND DEVELOPED AREAS OF AIRPORTS FOR WHICH THESE FIGURES WERE GIVEN (*Continued*)

Number of Airports Reporting Both 50

NAME	TOTAL ACREAGE	DEVELOPED ACREAGE
LOUISVILLE	203	203
MACON	247	50
MEMPHIS	202	202
MIAMI		
Pan-American Airport	130	130
MILWAUKEE		
Milwaukee County Airport	305	160
MONTGOMERY	956	600
NEWARK	420	175
OAKLAND	845	845
PONTIAC	240	140
PORTLAND, ME.	193	90
RICHMOND	400	50
ROCHESTER	110	105
ST. LOUIS		
St. Louis Airport	300	100
SALISBURY	176	85
SCHENECTADY	199	90
TERRE HAUTE	162	115
TOLEDO		
Toledo Airport	225	160
Transcontinental Airport	515	160
UTICA	357	140
VALLEY STREAM	400	325
WAYNE COUNTY	640	440
WICHITA	640	390
WINSTON-SALEM	100	52
	Average Total Acreage, 361.8	Average Developed Acreage, 211.1

APPENDIX 10

COSTS OF CLEARING, GRADING, AND DRAINING MUNICIPAL AIRPORTS[1]

A. Costs of Clearing

Name	Total Cost	Number of Acres Developed	Cost per Acre
Akron [2]	$ 19,000.00	80	$237.50
Albany	100,000.00	235	425.53
Buffalo	100,000.00	200	500.00
Des Moines	1,036.49	160	6.48
Kansas City, Mo.	13,000.00	400	32.50
Louisville	200.00	203	0.99
Minneapolis	163,000.00	325	501.54
Pontiac	3,026.78	140	21.62
Richmond	5,000.00	50	100.00
Syracuse	3,491.76	132	26.45
Wayne County	41,720.00	440	94.82
Total	$449,475.03	2365	Average cost per acre, $190.05

[1] Figures obtained for these items on commercial ports are confidential and therefore cannot be given.

[2] For the name of the airport in each case, see Appendix 1, List of Airports Visited.

COSTS OF CLEARING, GRADING, AND DRAINING
MUNICIPAL AIRPORTS (*Continued*)

B. Costs of Grading

NAME	TOTAL COST	NUMBER OF ACRES DEVELOPED	COST PER ACRE
AKRON	$737,000.00	80	$9212.50
ALBANY	178,500.00	235	759.57
BUFFALO	30,000.00	200	150.00
CINCINNATI	75,000.00	450	166.67
DES MOINES	7,506.31	160	46.91
FORT WORTH	8,000.00	213	37.56
KANSAS CITY, MO.	42,662.36	400	106.66
MINNEAPOLIS	15,000.00	325	46.15
MONTGOMERY	15,000.00	600	25.00
PONTIAC	4,719.75	140	33.71
RICHMOND	13,600.00	50	272.00
ST. LOUIS	127,000.00 [1]	480	264.58
SPARTANBURG	4,000.00	105	38.10
SYRACUSE	32,285.59	132	244.59
TULSA	15,000.00	440	34.09
WAYNE COUNTY	48,405.00	440	110.01
WICHITA	2,500.00	384	6.51
TOTAL	$1,356,179.01	4834	Average cost per acre, $280.55

C. Costs of Clearing and Grading

NAME	TOTAL COST	NUMBER OF ACRES DEVELOPED	COST PER ACRE
COLUMBUS	$30,000.00 [2]	534	$56.18
DAYTON	13,500.00 [2]	310	43.55
TERRE HAUTE	2,000.00	115	17.39
TOLEDO	3,000.00	160	18.75
TOTAL	$48,500.00	1119	Average cost per acre, $43.34

[1] Includes diversion of creek.   [2] Includes cost of seeding.

D. Costs of Draining

NAME	TOTAL COST	NUMBER OF ACRES DEVELOPED	COST PER ACRE
AKRON	$70,000.00	80	$875.00
BUFFALO	29,000.00	200	145.00
CINCINNATI	5,000.00	450	11.11
COLUMBUS	75,000.00 [1]	534	140.45
DALLAS			
Love Field	250,000.00	173	1445.09
DAYTON	8,300.00 [2]	310	26.77
DES MOINES	1,051.80	160	6.57
KANSAS CITY, Mo.	23,984.15	400	59.96
PONCA CITY			
Everett Taylor Airport . .	200.00	80	2.50
PONTIAC	385.25	140	2.75
RICHMOND	6,300.00	50	126.00
ROCHESTER	3,232.39	105	30.78
ST. LOUIS	200,000.00	480	416.67
SYRACUSE	1,324.66	132	10.04
TULSA	5,000.00	440	11.36
WAYNE COUNTY	229,000.00	440	520.45
TOTAL	$907,778.25	4174	Average cost per acre, $217.49

E. Costs of Clearing, Grading, and Draining

NAME	TOTAL COST	NUMBER OF ACRES DEVELOPED	COST PER ACRE
CHICAGO	$129,000.00	160	$806.25
CLEVELAND	139,000.00	700	198.57
DETROIT	346,040.00	270	1281.63
TOTAL	$614,040.00	1130	Average cost per acre, $543.40

[1] Includes cost of sewerage.   [2] Includes cost of storm sewers.

APPENDIX 11

DIFFICULTIES DUE TO DEVELOPMENTS IN SURROUNDING AREAS

A. Height of Structures

Out of 83 airports 16 reported difficulties due to the height of structures outside the boundaries of the field. Types of structures mentioned include the following: buildings, oil tanks, power transmission lines, radio towers, a railroad trestle, and trees.

B. Smoke

Out of 83 airports 12 reported difficulties due to the presence of smoke.

C. Nuisances

Out of 83 airports 12 reported the development of such nuisances as hot-dog stands and billboards, but five of these airports said that the number of such structures was not yet serious.

APPENDIX 12

AREAS WITHIN A TWENTY–MINUTE RADIUS OF THE HEART OF THE CITY BY PRESENT MEANS OF TRANSPORTATION, WHICH ARE STILL AVAILABLE FOR AIRPORT SITES

Fifty-nine cities reported as follows: 15, reported none; 6, very few; 4, one; 4, two; 4, three; 2, four; 3, six; 21, many.

APPENDIX 13

WATER AREAS AND PLANS WHICH HAVE BEEN MADE TO USE THEM AS SEAPLANE BASES

AKRON. Springfield Lake, adjacent to port, is not considered at present safe for seaplane operation.

ALAMEDA. Many areas along San Francisco Bay. If completed according to present plans, Alameda Airport will be combined landplane and seaplane base.

ALBANY. Areas along Hudson River in South Albany. No plans made to use them. Airport is $7\frac{1}{2}$ miles from river harbor.

ARLINGTON. The Potomac River borders Hoover Field and Washington Airport. No definite plans to use it.

ATCHISON. The airport, $\frac{1}{4}$ mile from the Missouri River, adjoins Sugar Lake, which has an area of 400 acres. Future plans contemplate combination landplane and seaplane base.

ATLANTIC CITY. Water areas available for seaplane ports. Plans to use them discussed.

BOSTON. Airport flanked by harbor. Seaplane base suggested on harbor side of airport.

BUFFALO. City holds waterfront land which Department of Public Works plans to utilize for seaplane port.

CHICAGO. Areas along lakefront available. Numerous plans made to use them. At present there is small seaplane base on lakefront.

CINCINNATI. Two hundred acres at junction of Little Miami and Ohio rivers available for seaplane port, but no plans made to use them.

CLEVELAND. Areas on lakefront and at mouth of Rocky River available. Plans made to develop them as auxiliary landing areas and for seaplanes. Commercial operator considering shuttle service from lakefront to airport.

DETROIT. Studies to consider possibility of developing seaplane port along lakefront being initiated.

FORT WORTH. Lake Worth, $2\frac{1}{2}$ miles west of city, is normally too smooth for operation of seaplanes. No plans made to utilize it.

GLENVIEW. Amphibian shuttle service between lakefront and airport is in use when demand warrants it.

GROSSE ILE. Airport property adjoins Lake Erie and Detroit River. Naval seaplane port already developed next to airport.

HARTFORD. Water areas available on river near port. No definite plans made to utilize them. Problem of variation of 25 to 30 feet in water level would necessitate careful planning for hangars and ramps.

JACKSONVILLE. Areas available along St. Johns River. Indefinite plans made to use land already owned by city, near municipal docks, for seaplane base.

KANSAS CITY, KAN. Areas available along Missouri River. Seaplane base and recreation beach planned.

KANSAS CITY, MO. Shores of Missouri River available. No definite plans for seaplane base.

LOUISVILLE. Suitable areas available on river harbor. Plans for development of seaplane port not definite but sites are under consideration.

MEMPHIS. Areas along Mississippi River available except that a 36-foot variation in water level makes hangars and ramps almost impracticable.

MIAMI. Areas suitable for seaplane port available along Biscayne Bay. A 300-acre combination landplane and seaplane airport planned on Virginia Key. Plans sponsored by Department of Public Service and Municipal Aviation Board and approved by the War Department involve expensive fill. Financial conditions make it impossible to carry out plans at present. City has leased temporary site which is in use as seaplane base. Private corporation has also established one.

MILWAUKEE. Many suitable areas available adjacent to Lake Michigan. Temporary ramp used by seaplanes last summer.

MINNEAPOLIS. Areas available at barge terminal on Mississippi, 6 miles from the present airport and 2 miles from center of town. Plans to use Nicollet Island as future seaplane base.

MONTGOMERY. Alabama River flows through city, but there is some doubt as to possibility of using it as seaplane base.

NEWARK. Unlimited natural opportunities for seaplane port but no definite plans to use them. They will doubtless be used eventually.

OAKLAND. Many areas along San Leandro Bay available for seaplane bases. Seaplane base being developed as part of Oakland Airport. Block of 20 acres was obtained for this specific purpose and deep-water channel constructed to airport proper for use of speed boats carrying cargo and passengers between airport and bay cities. Channel also serves industrial area adjacent to airport.

PARKVILLE, Mo. Missouri River near town. No definite plans for seaplane base.

PHILADELPHIA. Provision made for seaplane base in plans for development of Hog Island as combined air, rail, and water terminal.

PINE BLUFF. Large lake used by seaplanes, but land adjoining not yet developed as seaplane base.

PONTIAC. Within radius of 5 miles are 25 lakes ranging in size from $\frac{1}{2}$ to 10 square miles. Preliminary plans made by private concerns to use some of lakes for seaplane bases.

PORTLAND, ME. Areas adjoining harbor available, but no plans made to use them. Private airport company lands seaplanes in harbor occasionally.

ROCHESTER. Areas along lakefront and series of bays available but no plans made to use them.

ST. JOSEPH, Mo. Airport is on river. No seaplane base developed.

ST. LOUIS. In connection with park and riverfront development, areas are available for seaplane base but none of sites developed. Current, undertow, ice, etc. render site directly on river unsatisfactory. Artificial bay is only solution.

ST. PAUL. Projected inland harbor development south of airport may be changed to seaplane base. Seaplane base of 298 acres in form of equilateral triangle with sides 3400 feet long has been proposed, adjoining the airport.

SALISBURY. Largest artificial lake in world available for seaplane port but no plans made to utilize it.

SAN FRANCISCO. Many available sites on San Francisco Bay but none developed.

SCHENECTADY. Sites along Mohawk River may possibly be suitable for seaplane base but no plans made to use them.

SPARTANBURG. Reservoir available for seaplanes but this use not contemplated.

SYRACUSE. Plans made for seaplane base on Onondaga Lake. Future development of plans assured.

TAMPA. Areas along harbor and bay available. Site for projected joint landplane and seaplane base selected.

TERRE HAUTE. Land along river available. Combined landplane and seaplane base proposed.

TOLEDO. Plan to build combination landplane and seaplane port on waterfront.

WESTON, Mo. Present airport $\frac{1}{2}$ mile from river. No plans to use it for seaplanes.

APPENDIX 14

AIRPORTS AT VARIOUS DISTANCES FROM NEAREST STEAM RAILROAD PASSENGER STATION ON A MAIN LINE

Number of Airports Reporting 74

DISTANCE IN MILES	NUMBER OF AIRPORTS	DISTANCE IN MILES	NUMBER OF AIRPORTS
0. to 0.5 [1]	6	5.1 to 6	4
0.6 to 1	3	6.1 to 7	10
1.1 to 2	16	7.1 to 8	6
2.1 to 3	13	8.1 to 9	2
3.1 to 4	7	9.1 to 10	1
4.1 to 5	6		

[1] In only one case was there a main-line railroad passenger station directly at the port.

APPENDIX 15

AIRPORTS AT VARIOUS DISTANCES FROM NEAREST FREIGHT STATION ON A MAIN LINE

Number of Airports Reporting 75

DISTANCE IN MILES	NUMBER OF AIRPORTS	DISTANCE IN MILES	NUMBER OF AIRPORTS
0. to 0.5 [1]	14	5.1 to 6	1
0.6 to 1	7	6.1 to 7	7
1.1 to 2	17	7.1 to 8	6
2.1 to 3	6	8.1 to 9	1
3.1 to 4	11		
4.1 to 5	5		

[1] In only two cases was there a main-line freight station practically adjacent to the airport.

APPENDIX 16

AIRPORTS AND TRANSPORTATION TIME FROM BUSINESS CENTERS OF CITIES

Number of Airports Reporting 79

Time in Minutes	Number of Airports	Time in Minutes	Number of Airports
0 to 5	6	21 to 25	10
6 to 10	11	26 to 30	10
11 to 15	13	31 to 35	3
16 to 20	15	36 to 40	2
		41 to 45	7
		60	1
		90	1

APPENDIX 17

AIRPORTS AT VARIOUS DISTANCES FROM BUSINESS CENTERS OF CITIES

Number of Airports Reporting 81

Miles	Number of Airports	Miles	Number of Airports
0. to 1	4	10.1 to 11	1
1.1 to 2	13	11.1 to 12	2
2.1 to 3	9	12.1 to 13	2
3.1 to 4	4	13.1 to 14	1
4.1 to 5	6	14.1 to 15	1
5.1 to 6	7	15.1 to 16	1
6.1 to 7	9	16.1 to 17	0
7.1 to 8	10	17.1 to 18	1
8.1 to 9	5	18.1 to 19	2
9.1 to 10	2	19.1 to 20	0
		20.1 to 21	1

APPENDIX 18

TRANSIT SERVICE TO AIRPORTS[1]

Frequency of Service in Minutes	Kind of Service (Figures indicate the number of airports reporting this service)			
	Airport-Owned Busses	Common-Carrier Busses	Street Railways	Rapid Transit
5		1	2	1
10		3	3	
15		4	1	1
20		3		
25				
30		5	5	2
35				
40		1		
45		1		1
50				1
55				
60	3	12	2	8
180		3		
240		1		
Total Number	3	34	13	14

[1] 33 airports were served by taxicabs only.

APPENDIX 19

IMPEDIMENTS TO HIGHWAY TRAVEL BETWEEN AIRPORT AND CENTER OF CITY

A. Traffic Congestion

Out of 81 airports reporting, 51 reported traffic congestion as an impediment.

B. Railroad Grade Crossings

Out of 80 airports reporting, 52 reported railroad grade crossings as an impediment.

C. Poor Handling of Traffic

Out of 75 airports reporting, 6 reported poor handling of traffic, and 12 reported only fair handling of traffic.

D. Roads of Inadequate Width or Poorly Paved

Out of 83 airports reporting, 27 reported roads of inadequate width or poorly paved as an impediment.

E. Ferry Crossings or Drawbridges

Out of 80 airports, 5 reported one or the other of these as an impediment.

APPENDIX 20

WIDTH OF ANNOYANCE FRINGE AROUND AN AIRPORT

Out of 55 airports reporting, 29 airports replied that an annoyance fringe definitely existed and estimated its depth as follows:

9 estimated its depth as not exceeding $\frac{1}{4}$ mile
13 estimated its depth as not exceeding $\frac{1}{2}$ mile
5 estimated its depth as not exceeding 1 mile
1 estimated its depth as not exceeding 2 miles
1 estimated its depth as not exceeding 10 miles

8 airports reported that an annoyance fringe existed but that its depth was indefinite.

5 said that the annoyance fringe was temporary, and 13 said that an annoyance fringe did not exist.

The following comments were interesting:

"People who live about are poor and don't complain."

"It is merely a matter of becoming accustomed to the annoyance."

"Annoyance fringe ends at end of runways."

162

APPENDIX 21

OBJECTIONS TO AIRPORTS MADE BY THOSE LIVING IN THEIR VICINITY

A. Noise

Out of 82 airports, 17 reported receiving complaints against noise. Five said that these complaints were of a minor character. The following comments on this subject were made:

The complaints were a result of low flying.

The complaint was made because the owner wanted the city to buy his property.

A great many complaints have been received but all the testimony is exaggerated.

A petition signed by fifty people requested the reduction of noise.

Complaints have been received from a high-class residential district two or three miles from the airport.

A church complained against the noise on Sunday, and poultry raisers have complained that the airplanes frighten their chickens.

B. Dust

Out of 82 airports, 11 reported receiving complaints against dust, but most of the complaints were received during construction operations.

C. Night Lighting

Few complaints against annoyance caused by night lighting of airports were reported. Most of the complaints reported were a result of faulty adjustment of lights. One airport reported a complaint from a hospital before the lighting equipment was put into operation. They feared that the beacon light would disturb their patients.

D. Danger

Out of 82 airports, 17 had received complaints against the operation of the airport because of the danger to those living in the surrounding territory; seven of those complaints were primarily against low flying.

The manager of one airport reported that he had received no complaints on the score of danger, but that insurance companies in the city were selling a great many policies providing protection against property damage caused by falling aircraft or aircraft equipment.

163

APPENDIX 22

THE EFFECT OF THE AIRPORT ON LAND VALUES

AKRON.[1] Caused abnormal inflation of prices.

ALAMEDA. Increased values tremendously. Before establishment of airport, land had very low value.

ALBANY. Increased price and sale.

ARLINGTON

    Hoover Field. Increased land values.

    Washington Airport. Will increase land values.

ATLANTA. Effect not determined. Land immediately adjacent to airport undesirable for residential purposes.

ATLANTIC CITY. Increased residential property sales.

BOSTON. No definite effect as yet.

BUFFALO. Increased price. Very little increase in sales.

CHARLOTTE. Depreciated values slightly.

CHICAGO. Has decreased sales, but not property values.

CINCINNATI. Land prices more than doubled. Little increase in actual number of sales.

CLEVELAND

    Cleveland Airport. Decreased land values.

    Curtiss-Herrick Airport. Prices and number of sales have increased.

DALLAS.

    Curtiss-Wright Airport. Land values increase 20 per cent.

    Hensley Field. Land values doubled.

    Love Field. Increased land values considerably.

DAYTON. Increased sale price but not the number of sales.

DES MOINES. Use of land as homesites for airport personnel has increased its value. Otherwise it would be used only as farm land.

DETROIT. No noticeable effect.

FORT WORTH. Increased values 25 to 30 per cent.

GARDEN CITY. Increased some values and decreased others. In general, has increased value of undeveloped land and has not lowered residential values.

GLENDALE. Increased value of adjoining property because it created a demand for factory sites in that locality.

GLENVIEW. No change traceable to the airport as yet noticeable.

GROSSE ILE. Number of sales of adjoining property increased, but the price has remained about the same.

[1] For name of airport in each case, see Appendix 1, List of Airports Visited.

164

HARTFORD. Greatly increased land prices.

INDIANAPOLIS

Capitol Airways Airport. Increased sale of property.

Hoosier Airport. No effect.

Indianapolis Airport. Increased price of land but not the number of sales.

Stout Field. Price but not land values increased.

JACKSONVILLE. No effect.

KANSAS CITY, KAN. Prices doubled but no sale for land.

KANSAS CITY, MO. Increased values.

LOS ANGELES

Metropolitan Airport. Slightly increased values.

Mines Field. Increased both values and sales.

Western Air Express Terminal. Slightly increased values.

LOUISVILLE. No effect on land values.

MACON. No definite effect as yet.

MEMPHIS. No definite effect as yet.

MIAMI

Miami Airport. Land improved by structures has increased in value because of demand for housing facilities for airport personnel.

Pan-American Airport. Increased values 200 per cent.

MILWAUKEE

Curtiss-Milwaukee Airport. Airport tends to increase land values for one year and then they sink back to normal.

Maitland Field. The development of the lake port as a whole has increased land values. The airport itself has done little to increase land values.

Milwaukee County. Tended to increase land values.

MINNEAPOLIS. Land being held for increased price but there is no market for it.

MONTGOMERY. Increased values considerably.

NEWARK. No effect.

OAKLAND. Probably increased values due partly to development of adjacent land as industrial sites.

ORANGE. Increased land values on bordering properties.

PHILADELPHIA. Slightly increased values.

PINE BLUFF. Slight increase in values.

PONCA CITY. No increase in values.

PONTIAC. Increased prices and to some extent number of sales.

PORTLAND, ME. No increase in values.

RICHMOND. Increase in price of land immediately surrounding airport.

ROCHESTER. Increased price but not sales.

ST. JOSEPH. No increase in values.

ST. LOUIS

Curtiss-Steinberg Field. Increased values.

St. Louis Airport. No effect on values.

ST. PAUL. Land values doubled since city started to acquire land for airport.

SALISBURY. Some increase in land values.

SAN FRANCISCO. Materially increased values.

SCHENECTADY. Increased land prices but not sales. Increased price of additional acreage which airport wishes to obtain.

SPARTANBURG. Slightly increased ability to sell property for specialized uses.

SYRACUSE. Increased prices 30 per cent but not sales.

TAMPA. No change in values.

TERRE HAUTE. No change in values.

TOLEDO

Toledo Airport. Slight increase in values. Some stimulation of sales.

Transcontinental Airport. Price increased but no sales have been made.

TULSA. Increased values.

UTICA. Price increased 100 per cent but number of sales has not.

VALLEY STREAM. Slight increase in land values.

WAYNE COUNTY. Impossible to determine effect of airport at present.

WESTON, MO. No increase in values.

WICHITA. Tripled value of land.

WINSTON-SALEM. No effect.

APPENDIX 23

AIRPORTS BUILT ON PARK LANDS

In answer to the question, "Has the airport been built on park lands," out of eighty-two replies only the following affirmative answers were received:

DES MOINES.[1] Was originally called Des Moines Airport Park in order to operate under existing state laws. An enabling act passed last year gave city power to acquire, maintain, and operate an airport.

DETROIT. Airport built on land legally a park, but used as a dump.

LOUISVILLE. Airport site purchased as park land.

MIAMI

Miami Dirigible Airport. Land given to be used as both dirigible airport and golf course.

Miami Seaplane Base. Airport built on water reserve land.

MILWAUKEE

Maitland Field. Airport built on what was originally submerged land set aside for park purposes by State of Wisconsin and later turned over for harbor purposes.

MONTGOMERY. Airport is classed as park. Was acquired under state statute permitting acquisition of park land beyond corporate limits.

ST. PAUL. Small portion of land used as airport site was originally given by subdivider to city for recreational purposes.

SPARTANBURG. Land bought as park land but for use as airport. Was called an air park in resolution authorizing purchase.

TULSA. If city purchases the airport, they will take it as a park.

WICHITA. Airport designated legally as a park.

[1] For name of airport in each case, see Appendix 1, List of Airports Visited.

APPENDIX 24

OPINIONS ON THE PUBLIC OWNERSHIP OF AIRPORTS

Opinion of 38 Municipal Airport Officials

For Municipal Ownership 29
Against Municipal Ownership . . . 2
Undecided 5
For Municipal Ownership with Private
  Operation 2

Opinion of 12 Commercial Airport Officials

For Municipal Ownership 4
Against Municipal Ownership . . . 6
Undecided 0
For Municipal Ownership with Private
  Operation 2

OPINIONS ON COUNTY OWNERSHIP OF AIRPORTS

Opinion of 2 County Airport Officials
For County Ownership 2

APPENDIX 25

MUNICIPALITIES WHERE AIRPORTS ARE OUTSIDE THE CORPORATE LIMITS

ALBANY
ATLANTA
BUFFALO
CLEVELAND
COLUMBUS
DES MOINES
FORT WORTH
INDIANAPOLIS
JACKSONVILLE
KANSAS CITY, MO.
LOUISVILLE
MACON
MEMPHIS
MIAMI

MINNEAPOLIS
MONTGOMERY
PONCA CITY
PONTIAC
RICHMOND
ROCHESTER
ST. JOSEPH
ST. LOUIS
SALISBURY
SAN FRANCISCO
SPARTANBURG
SYRACUSE
TAMPA
TOLEDO

APPENDIX 26

CITIES WHERE THE AIRPORT IS SEPARATELY ADMINISTERED

A. BY THE AVIATION DEPARTMENT UNDER A SINGLE EXECUTIVE:

DALLAS. Commission Government. Director appointed for one year by mayor with consent of the commission.

FORT WORTH. Commission-Manager Government. Director appointed for one year by city manager with consent of the commission.

LOS ANGELES. Mayor-Council. Director selected by council from three candidates receiving highest grades in the Civil Service examination.

MIAMI. Commission-Manager Government. Director appointed for one year by city manager with consent of the commission.

PONCA CITY. Mayor-Council-Manager. Director appointed for an indefinite term by mayor with consent of the council.

PONTIAC. Commission-Manager. Director appointed by city manager with approval of the commission (none appointed as yet).

B. BY THE AVIATION DEPARTMENT UNDER A BOARD:

HARTFORD. Name: Air Board. Six members appointed for six years by mayor with approval of the council. Two members every year. No salary.

LOUISVILLE. Name: Louisville and Jefferson County Air Board. Six members appointed for four years by mayor and county judge, all terms expiring simultaneously. Three Republicans, three Democrats.

MEMPHIS. Name: Airport Commission. Five members appointed for one year by mayor. No salary.

SALISBURY. Name: Airport Commission. Three members. One city representative and two citizens appointed for an indefinite period by council.

TERRE HAUTE. Name: Board of Aviation Commissioners. Four members appointed for four years by mayor, one retiring annually. Two Republicans, two Democrats.

WINSTON-SALEM. Name: Miller Municipal Airport Commission, representing the Winston-Salem Foundation. Five members: mayor, chairman of the Board of County Commissioners, president of the Chamber of Commerce, and two citizens.

C. BY A COUNCIL COMMITTEE:

ATLANTA. Five members

MACON. Three members

SAN FRANCISCO. Three members

APPENDIX 27

CITIES WHERE THE DEPARTMENT OF PUBLIC WORKS IS IN CHARGE OF THE AIRPORT

ALBANY
CHICAGO (Bureau of Parks, Recreation and Aviation)
DETROIT
INDIANAPOLIS
KANSAS CITY, Mo.

PHILADELPHIA
RICHMOND
ROCHESTER
TAMPA
UTICA

APPENDIX 28

CITIES WHERE THE DEPARTMENT OF PARKS IS IN CHARGE OF THE AIRPORT

ATLANTIC CITY
BOSTON
BUFFALO
CLEVELAND
DES MOINES

MINNEAPOLIS
ST. LOUIS
SPARTANBURG
SYRACUSE
WICHITA

APPENDIX 29

CITIES WHERE THE DEPARTMENT OF PUBLIC SERVICE IS IN CHARGE OF THE AIRPORT

AKRON
CINCINNATI

COLUMBUS
TOLEDO

APPENDIX 30

CITIES AND COUNTIES WHERE THE AIRPORT IS ADMINISTERED BY OTHER DEPARTMENTS

JACKSONVILLE. Department of Radio Station and Highway
MILWAUKEE. Harbor Board
MILWAUKEE COUNTY. Highway Committee of the County Board
MONTGOMERY. Commission of Public Works and Parks
NEWARK. Department of Public Affairs (Port Newark Development)
OAKLAND. Board of Port Commissioners
ST. PAUL. Department of Public Utilities
WAYNE COUNTY. Road Commission

APPENDIX 31

CITIES WHICH PROVIDE AIRPORT ADVISORY BOARDS

AKRON. Name: Airport Committee. Mayor appoints, council approves, 3 members
Service Director, Chairman
1 member selected by President of Goodyear Zeppelin Company
President of University of Akron

ALBANY. Name: Air Board. Mayor appoints, council affirms, 7 members for one year
Commissioner of Public Works
Corporation Counsel
Mayor
Secretary
3 citizens

ATLANTIC CITY. Name: Advisory Board. Mayor appoints 6 members for five years
Mayor
Commissioner
2 members of School Board
2 members to represent citizens

BOSTON. Name: Citizens Advisory Board. Mayor appoints a varying number of members, usually 5

BUFFALO. Name: Airport Advisory Board. Commissioner of Parks appoints 5 members for the period of his administration

CHICAGO. Name: Aero Commission. Mayor appoints 12 members for four years with consent of council
3 must be aldermen (one of these a member of the council committee on aviation)
9 citizens

DALLAS.   Name: Board of Air Control. Mayor appoints 5 members for
               two years with approval of council.
               Street Commissioner one of the members
               4 residents of the city
MIAMI.   Name: Municipal Aviation Board. City Manager appoints 5 mem-
               bers for one year with the approval of the commission. No
               qualifications
PHILADELPHIA. Name: Board of Control. 3 members
               1 from City Property Department
               1 from National Guard
               1 from Ludington Philadelphia Flying Service
ST. LOUIS.   Name: City Air Board. 10 members
               5 citizens appointed by Mayor for indefinite term
               5 city officials: President of the Board of Aldermen, and 4 officials
               representing departments of Law, Finance, Welfare, and Parks
ST. PAUL.   Name: Advisory Board. 10 members
               7 citizens selected from the "Greater St. Paul Committee" by the
               Mayor for an indefinite period. No qualifications
               3 council members representing the departments of Public Works,
               Utilities, and Committee of Education
SAN FRANCISCO. Name: Citizens' Airport Advisory Board. Supervisors' Airport Com-
               mittee appoints 3 members for the term of the supervisors
SYRACUSE.   Name: Mayor's Advisory Board. From 14 to 24 members appointed
               by the Mayor for an indefinite period. No qualifications

171

APPENDIX 32

CITIES WHICH LEASE THEIR AIRPORT FOR PRIVATE OPERATION

MACON
MONTGOMERY
PHILADELPHIA

RICHMOND
ST. JOSEPH
SPARTANBURG
WINSTON-SALEM

APPENDIX 33

AVERAGE COST OF LAND PER ACRE AT 30 MUNICIPAL AIRPORTS AND 15 COMMERCIAL AIRPORTS

Average cost of land per acre at 30 municipal airports and 15 commercial airports $974.28

Average number of acres at 30 municipal airports and 15 commercial airports 396⅓ acres

Average cost per acre at 30 municipal airports $713.50

Average number of acres at 30 municipal airports . . . . 415⅔ acres

Average cost per acre at 15 commercial airports $1495.80

Average number of acres at 15 commercial airports . . . . 357⅔ acres

APPENDIX 34

COST OF ACREAGE AND NUMBER OF ACRES AT 30 MUNICIPAL AIRPORTS

	Cost	Acres
Akron	$ 1155.00	829
Atlanta	320.00	300
Atlantic City	2649.00	300
Buffalo	807.00	555
Cincinnati	350.00	760
Cleveland	1200.00	1085
Columbus	561.00	534
Dallas		
Hensley Field	157.00	285
Love Field	2167.00	173
Fort Worth	750.00	225
Hartford	1086.00	425
Indianapolis	292.00	915
Kansas City, Mo.	1294.00	687
Macon	50.00	247
Milwaukee County	486.00	320
Minneapolis	580.00	325
Montgomery	104.00	965
Pontiac	648.00	240
Richmond	75.00	100
Rochester	454.00	110
St. Louis	2000.00	480
St. Paul	400.00	300
Salisbury	151.00	176
Spartanburg	183.00	105
Syracuse	408.00	132
Terre Haute	496.00	162
Utica	230.00	357
Wayne County	1252.00	640
Wichita	100.00	640
Winston-Salem	1000.00	100
	$21,405.00	12,472

APPENDIX 35

COMMERCIAL AIRPORTS WHICH LEASE THEIR LAND

Alameda Airport, Alameda . . . . 346 acres
Atchison Airport, Atchison . . . . 167 acres
Capitol Airport, Indianapolis . . . . 176 acres
Hoosier Airport, Indianapolis . . . . 80 acres
Weston Field, Weston . . . . 160 acres

APPENDIX 36

MUNICIPALITIES WHICH LEASE LAND FOR AIRPORT SITES

City	Lessor	Number of Acres	Cost per Annum	Yearly Cost per Acre	Length of Lease	Privilege of Renewal	Option to Buy
Albany	County	235	$1		10 yrs.	For 10 yrs.	No
Boston	Commonwealth of Mass.	131	$1		10 yrs.	Undecided	No
Chicago	Board of Education, Chicago	320	$6400	$20.00			
Des Moines . .	Private Owner	160	$3900	$24.37	5 yrs.	No	At $400 per acre
Fort Worth . . (a portion of airport)		200	$1000	$5.00	5 yrs.	Yes	At $750 per acre
Los Angeles . .	Private Owner	640	$96,000 for first year. For 9 years, $126,000	$192.18			5-yr. option at $300 an acre
Louisville . . .	Board of Park Commissioners	203	$1		10 yrs.	Yes	No
Memphis . . .	Private Owner	202	$1200	$59.40	7 yrs.	Yes	At $500 an acre
Ponca City . .	State of Oklahoma	320	$11,000 for 99 years and $240 a year		99 yrs.	Yes	No
Richmond . . .	Private Owner	300	$1800	$6.00	5 yrs.	For 2 yrs.	At $75 per acre
San Francisco .	Private Owner	170	$1500	$8.82	3 yrs.	Yes	Yes
Tampa	Private Owner	240	Remission of taxes, $700 and all concession rights		3 yrs.	Yes	Yes
Toledo	Private Owner	225	$1125	$5.00	3 yrs.	For 2 yrs.	No

Total cost for eight cities [1] per acre $320.77
Average yearly cost per city per acre . . . . $ 40.09

[1] Cities paying nominal charge for acreage are omitted in calculations.

APPENDIX 37

COST OF MAINTENANCE AND OPERATION PER FISCAL YEAR AT MUNICIPAL AIRPORTS

City	Year	Cost (1930 cost estimated)
Akron	1929	$ 12,700
Albany	1929	30,000
Atlanta	1930	15,000 [1]
Buffalo	1929	95,000
Chicago	1929	42,000 [1]
Cincinnati	1930	20,000
Cleveland	1929	29,000 [1]
Columbus	1929	15,500 [1]
Dallas	1929	12,000 [1]
Des Moines	1930	4,000
Detroit	1930	112,000
Fort Worth	1930	16,000 [1]
Hartford	1929	44,358 [1]
Kansas City, Mo.	1930	100,000
Louisville	1930	31,100
Macon (Port leased)	1929	2,000 [1]
Miami	1929	10,000 [1]
Milwaukee	1929	13,130
Minneapolis	1929	14,134
Oakland	1929	25,000
Pontiac	1929	25,530
Richmond (Port leased)	1929	2,000
Rochester	1929	40,550
St. Louis	1929	36,000
St. Paul	1928	26,391
Spartanburg	1929	7,000
Tampa	1930	18,000
Terre Haute	1930	12,000
Toledo	1929	7,000 [1]
Utica	1929	12,000 [1]
Milwaukee County	1927	9,236
		$838,629 Total
		$ 27,052.54 Average

[1] Amounts actually appropriated for that year. In other cities appropriations actually made were less than the estimated maintenance and operation cost by the amount of the estimated revenue. In a few cities the appropriation exceeded the maintenance cost to permit capital expenditures.

175

THE LAW OF AIRPORTS

REFERENCES

No attempt is made here to give references with any completeness to the authorities in support of general statements of law, such references as are given being suggestive rather than exhaustive. Nor as a rule have the authorities with regard to the general principles of aviation law been cited. The United States Government, through the Aeronautical Division of the Department of Commerce, furnishes information with regard to all phases of aeronautics on request. Especially valuable, perhaps, on the law is "Civil Aeronautics, Legislative History of the Air Commerce Act of 1926, together with miscellaneous legal materials relating to Civil Air Navigation," the latest edition being corrected to August 1, 1928. A collection of the laws and decisions on aviation is United States Aviation Reports, published in Baltimore annually, beginning in 1928. A bibliography of aviation, by Rudolph Hirschberg, will be found in the June, 1929, number (Vol. II., No. 5) of the *Southern California Law Review*, a quarterly published by the School of Law of the University of Southern California at Los Angeles. The latest American book on aviation law is Davis's "Aeronautical Law," published by Parker, Stone and Baird Company, Los Angeles.

In this report and appendix the endeavor has been made to include important statutes up to the close of the year 1929, and important decisions appearing up to July 1, 1930.

38. In this explanation use has been made of what the writer has already said in a lecture in a City Planning course at Harvard University, March 30, 1928, as printed in *City Planning* for July, 1928.

39. State *ex rel.* Oliver Cadillac Co. *v.* Christopher, 317 Mo. 1179 at 1192.

40. "The Law of City Planning and Zoning," by Frank B. Williams. New York, The Macmillan Co., 1922, p. 25.

41. An excellent brief presentation of the law on this phase of the subject is "Law of Aerial Navigation, Document No. 221, Senate of U. S. 70th Congress, 2d Session."

42. Arizona, see General Order No. 113-L. of the Arizona Corporation Commission, dated Nov. 10, 1928, given in 1929 U. S. Aviation Rep., p. 409.
California, Michigan, North Carolina, see decisions cited in note 44, below.
Nevada, see Rule No. 9, Feb. 5, 1929, given in 1929 U. S. Aviation Rep., p. 668.

43. Pennsylvania, 1929, No. 316, secs. 1202–1208.

44. California, Western Association of
    Railroads *v.* Railroad Com-
    mission, 173 Calif. 802.

Michigan, *Re* Air Taxi Service,
    Inc., Public Utility Reports,
    1927, D 279.

Nevada, *Re* Francis A. Riorden,
    P. U. R. 1928, D 854.

North Carolina, Bureau of Light-
    houses *v.* Southern Pub. Ut.
    Co., P. U. R. 1928, E 307.

Pennsylvania, *Re* Gettysburg Fly-
    ing Service, Inc., P. U. R.
    1928, B 287; Application of
    Battlefield Airways, Inc.,
    P. U. R. 1929, A 476, 1929
    U. S. Av. Rep. 54.

But see Colorado, *Re* U. S. Air-
    ways, Inc., P. U. R. 1928, E
    518.

45. On Littleton, 4*a.*

46. A good statement of the authorities on this phase of the subject is to be found in *Civil Aeronautics* (corrected to August 1, 1928), a pamphlet printed by the United States for the use of the Committee on Interstate and Foreign Commerce of the House of Representatives. After giving the foreign law to some extent this pamphlet, on page 86, continues :

> This ancient maxim [*cujus est solum* etc.] finds a limited survival in some American State codes, as, for example, that of Calif. Civ. Code (sec. 829), which provides that "the owner of land in fee has the right to the surface and to everything permanent situated beneath or above it."
>
> But, notwithstanding the persistence of this rule, its application to the space not immediately adjacent to the soil and the structures on the soil is wanting. All the decisions are regarding intrusions into the space very near the surface, where the actual use of the soil by the surface occupant was disturbed. It is believed that an examination of the cases will show that *cujus est solum* is not law, but is merely a nice theory, easily passed down from medieval days, because there has not been until recently any occasion to apply it to its full extent.
>
> It has been held to be a trespass to thrust one's arm into the space over a neighbor's land (Hannabalson *v.* Sessions, 116 Iowa, 457 (1902)) or to shoot over another's land (Whittaker *v.* Stangvick, 100 Minn. 386 (1907)), and for one's horse to kick into such space (Ellis *v.* Loftus Iron Co., 10 C. P. (Eng.) 10 (1874)). Overhanging branches constitute a legal wrong, either a trespass or a nuisance (Lemmon *v.* Webb, 1895 App. Cas. 1; Smith *v.* Giddy (1904), 2 K. B. 448; Grandona *v.* Lovdal, 70 Calif. 161 (1886); Tanner *v.* Wallbrunn, 77 Mo. App. 262 (1898); Ackerman *v.* Ellis, 81 N. J. L. 1 (1911); Countryman *v.* Lighthill, 24 Hun (N. Y.) 405 (1881)). A board attached to defendant's building and overhanging plaintiff's land constitutes a trespass (Puorto *v.* Chieppa, 78 Conn. 401 (1905); *contra,* Pickering *v.* Rudd, 4 Camp. (Eng.) 219 (1815)). In Pickering *v.* Rudd, Lord Ellenborough said (p. 221) : "Nay, if this board overhanging the plaintiff's garden be a trespass, it would follow that an aeronaut is liable to an action of trespass *quare clausum fregit* at the suit of the occupier of every field over which his balloon passes in the course of his voyage." This result Lord Ellenborough did not approve, but Blackburn, J., in Kenyon *v.* Hart (6 Best & Smith, (Eng.) 249, 251 (1865)), remarked : "I understand the good sense of that doubt, though not the legal reason of it."

So also projecting eaves (Harrington *v.* McCarthy, 169 Mass. 492 (1897); Aiken *v.* Benedict, 39 Barb. (N. Y.) 400 (1863); Huber *v.* Start, 124 Wis. 359 (1905)), cornices (Wilmarth *v.* Woodcock, 58 Mich. 482 (1885); Lawrence *v.* Hough, 35 N. J. Eq. 371 (1882); Crocker *v.* Manhattan Life Ins. Co., 61 App. Div. (N. Y.) 226 (1901)), roofs (Murphy *v.* Bolger, 60 Vt., 723 (1888)), and walls (Barnes *v.* Berendes, 139 Cal. 32 (1903); Norwalk Heating & Lighting Co. *v.* Vernan, 75 Conn. 662 (1903); Langfeldt *v.* McGrath, 33 Ill. App. 158 (1889); Codman *v.* Evans, 7 Allen (Mass.), 431 (1863); Lyle *v.* Littel, 83 Hun (N. Y.) 532 (1895), have been held to be wrongful and to give rise to an action of some sort. In Butler *v.* Frontier Telephone Co. (186 N. Y., 486 (1906)) it was held that ejectment would lie for the space occupied by a telephone wire strung across plaintiff's land at a height varying from 20 to 30 feet. Vann, J., expressed himself as follows:

"The surface of the ground is a guide, but not the full measure, for within reasonable limitations land includes not only the surface but also the space above and the part beneath. * * * *Usque ad coelum* is the upper boundary, and while this may not be taken too literally, there is no limitation within the bounds of any structure yet erected by man. So far as the case before us is concerned the plaintiff as the owner of the soil owned upward to an indefinite extent. * * * According to fundamental principles and within the limitation mentioned space above land is real estate the same as the land itself. * * * Unless the principle of *usque ad coelum* is abandoned, any physical, exclusive, and permanent occupation of space above land is an occupation of the land itself and a disseisin of the owner to that extent."

The English cases show that the stringing of a wire across land at low heights (30 to 34 feet) is regarded as a trespass (Finchley Elec. Lt. Co. *v.* Finchley Urban Dist. Council (1902), 1 Ch. 866 (1903), 1 Ch. 437; Wandsworth Board *v.* United Tel. Co., 13 Q. B. 904 (1884)). Leading text writers agree in substance that, in the words of Pollock, "the scope of possible trespasses is limited by that of possible effective possession" (Pollock, Torts (10th ed.), 364; Salmond, Torts, 163; Chapin, Torts, 349).

The operation of subways and tunnel streets as far below the surface as 150 feet has been regarded as wrongful as against the surface owner, in the absence of purchase or condemnation of the right (Matter of New York, 160 App. Div. 29 (1913), affirmed, 212 N. Y. 547; Matter of Willcox, 213 N. Y. 218 (1914); Matter of New York, 215 N. Y. 109 (1915)).

It thus appears that the only rights in space which have actually been protected by the courts have been rights in space immediately adjacent to and connected with the surface. There are no decisions to the effect that it is a wrong against a landowner to interfere with the space over his land at such a height that the use of the surface is not affected in the slightest degree.

All the codes now in existence and all proposed codes, so far as known to the writer, treat the landowner's property in the space above his land as subject to a right of passage by aircraft. None of these codes requires condemnation of an aerial right of way and none provides that the mere flight through the space above shall constitute a trespass. * * * "

47. Portsmouth Harbor Land and Hotel Co. *v.* United States Supreme Court, Dec. 4, 1922, reported in 1928 U. S. Av. Rep. 26.

Johnson *v.* Curtiss N. W. Airplane Co. (Minnesota), reported in 28 U. S. Av. Rep. 42.

Com. *v.* Nevin and Smith (Pennsylvania), reported in U. S. Av. Rep. 39.

Cattle Frightened by Airplane (Decision of U. S. Compt. Gen., Oct. 20, 1923), reported in 1928 U. S. Av. Rep. 46; Smith *v.* New England Aircraft Co., Inc., (Mass.) 170 N. E. R. 385.

48. Many modern statutes have provisions with regard to the ownership of the air space, none of which have been passed upon, as yet, by our courts. These statutes are:

Arizona, 1929, ch. 38, sec. 9.	Pennsylvania, 1929, Act 317, sec. 4.
Minnesota, 1929, ch. 219, sec. 3.	Rhode Island, 1929, ch. 1435, sec. 3.
Missouri, 1929, p. 122, sec. 3.	South Carolina, 1929, ch. 189, sec.
Montana, 1929, ch. 17, sec. 6.	3.
New Jersey, 1929, ch. 311, sec. 3.	Wisconsin, 1929, ch. 348, sec. 3;
North Carolina, 1929, ch. 190, sec. 3.	stat. 1143.

49. Smith *v.* New England Aircraft Co., Inc., (Mass.) 170 N. E. R. 385.

50. Article on "Constitutional Law," 12 Corpus Juris, 909, notes 30 and 31; Miller *v.* Board of Public Works, 195 Calif. 477, at 484; Village of Euclid *v.* Ambler Co., 272 U. S. 365, at 386.

51. Douty *v.* Mayor of Baltimore, 155 Maryland 125.

State *ex rel.* City of Lincoln *v.* Johnson, 117 Neb. 301.

Stern *v.* Mayor and Aldermen of Jersey City, 150 Atl. 9.

Hesse *v.* Rath, 230 N. Y. S. 672; 249 N. Y. 435.

State *ex rel.* Hile *v.* City of Cleveland, 160 N. E. 241 (Ohio).

McClintock *v.* City of Roseburg, 127 Ore. 698.

See Clayton and Lambert Mfg. Co. *v.* City of Detroit, 34 Fed. (2d) 303.

These cases hold that the establishment of an airport is a legitimate municipal purpose and to be such it must be a public purpose.

52. Alaska, 1929, ch. 29, sec. 1; ch. 110, sec. 1.

Arizona, 1929, ch. 38, sec. 2.

Arkansas, 1929, No. 135, sec. 1.

California, 1927, ch. 169, secs. 1, 4; ch. 267 (No. 149), sec. 1; 1929, ch. 404, sec. 1; ch. 847, sec. 1; Polit. Code, sec. 4056–c.

Connecticut, 1929, ch. 236, sec. 1; ch. 281, sec. 1; Spec. Acts, 1929, No. 194, sec. 1 (Hartford); No. 266, sec. 1 (N. Haven).

Florida, 1929, ch. 13569, sec. 1; ch. 13574, sec. 1; Spec. Sess. 1929, Special Acts (Lauderville, Leesburg, Mariana, Melbourne, Miami, City of Ocala and County of Maria, Panama City, Perry, St. Petersburg, Stark, Tallahassee, Taylor County, Nauchula.)

Georgia, 1927, p. 779, sec. 4; Spec. Sess. 1929, Local Acts for City of Brunswick and County of Glynn, and City of Newman and Cometa County.

Hawaii, 1927, No. 238, sec. 2 (4).

Idaho, 1929, ch. 106, sec. 1; ch. 108, sec. 1; ch. 133, sec. 1; ch. 241, sec. 1.

Illinois, 1927, p. 297, sec. 1.

Indiana, 1920, p. 160, sec. 3838' *et seq.;* 1921, ch. 111, sec. 1; 1928, ch. 48, sec. 1; 1929, ch. 57, sec. 1.

Iowa, 1929, ch. 138, sec. 1.

Kansas, 1921, ch. 264, sec. 3–110; 1929, ch. 5, secs. 1, 3.

Kentucky, 1924, ch. 76, sec. 1; 1926, ch. 107, secs. 165–2, –3, –6; 1928, ch. 78, secs. 1, 7.

Louisiana, 1928, No. 5, sec. 2; No. 24, secs. 2, 3; No. 43, sec. 1.

Maryland, 1929, ch. 219, secs. 14, 15; ch. 220, sec. 2.

Massachusetts, 1928, ch. 350, sec. 1; G. L. ch. 40, sec. 5 (35).

Michigan, 1927, No. 182, secs. 1–5; 1929, No. 103, secs. 1, 6; No. 210, sec. 1.

Minnesota, 1923, ch. 34, sec. 669–3; 1927, ch. 62, sec. 1626–1; 1929, ch. 125, sec. 1; ch. 217, secs. 1, 2; ch. 379, sec. 1.

Mississippi, 1929, ch. 63, secs. 1, 2, 3.

Missouri, 1929, p. 276, sec. 1.

Montana, 1927, ch. 20, sec. 5039; 1929, ch. 108, sec. 1.

Nebraska, 1922, Comp. Stat., sec. 4607; 1929, ch. 35, sec. 1.

New Hampshire, 1929, ch. 90, sec. 1; Pub. L. 1929, ch. 42, sec. 68a.

New Jersey, 1928, ch. 101, secs. 1, 2; ch. 181, sec. 1; 1929, ch. 26, sec. 1; ch. 206, sec. 1; ch. 325, secs. 1, 2; ch. 350, secs. 1, 2.

New Mexico, 1929, ch. 53, secs. 1, 2; ch. 54, sec. 2112.

New York, 1928, ch. 647, secs. 350–354; 1929, ch. 16, sec. 353a; ch. 31, sec. 350.

North Carolina, 1929, ch. 87, secs.

2, 3, 4; ch. 170, sec. 1; ch. 171, sec. 1.

North Dakota, 1929, ch. 86, sec. 1.

Ohio, Gen. Code, 1926, sec. 3677.

Oklahoma, 1929, ch. 11, sec. 1; ch. 83; ch. 238, sec. 1; 1929, S. B. 214.

Oregon, 1921, ch. 45, sec. 10; 1929, House Jt. Res. No. 2; 1929, ch. 195, sec. 1.

Pennsylvania, 1923, No. 192, secs. 460 b–1, –3, –4; 1925, No. 328, secs. 460 c–1, –3; 1927, No. 250, sec. 2; No. 494, secs. 1, 3, 4; 1929, No. 318, sec. 1; No. 446, sec. 1; No. 484, sec. 4.

South Carolina, 1928, No. 919, sec. 1; 1929, No. 461, sec. 1; No. 538, sec. 1; No. 562, sec. 1.

South Dakota, 1929, ch. 71, secs. 1, 2.

Tennessee, Private Acts, 1929, chs. 408, 759.

Texas, 1929 (1st Sess.), ch. 83; ch. 281, sec. 1.

Vermont, 1929, No. 60, sec. 1.

Virginia, 1928, p. 1172.

Washington, 1925, ch. 42, secs. 1–2; 1929, ch. 93, sec. 1.

West Virginia, 1929, ch. 61, secs. 2, 5.

Wisconsin, Stat. 114.11; 67.04 (4); 1921, ch. 234; 1927, ch. 248; 1929, ch. 285, sec. 59.08 (11); ch. 318; ch. 348, sec. 3; ch. 464, sec. 1; ch. 521, sec. 1.

Wyoming, 1927, ch. 72, sec. 5; 1929, ch. 66, sec. 4.

53. Arizona, 1929, ch. 38, sec. 3.

Arkansas, 1929, No. 135, sec. 4.

Florida, 1929, ch. 13569, sec. 3.

Indiana, 1929, ch. 57, sec. 13.

Iowa, 1929, ch. 138, sec. 9.

Kansas, 1929, ch. 5, sec. 3.

Louisiana, 1928, No. 5, sec. 2; No. 24, sec. 2.

Massachusetts, 1928, ch. 350, sec. 1.

Maryland, 1929, ch. 219, sec. 16.

Michigan, 1927, No. 182, sec. 3; 1929, No. 103, sec. 3, 6; No. 210, sec. 3.

Minnesota, 1929, ch. 217, sec. 3; ch. 379, sec. 3.

Mississippi, 1929, ch. 63, sec. 3.

Missouri, 1929, p. 276, sec. 3.

Montana, 1929, ch. 108, sec. 2.

Nebraska, 1929, ch. 35, sec. 2.

New Hampshire, 1929, ch. 90, sec. 1.

New Jersey, 1929, ch. 325, sec. 3; ch. 350, secs. 1, 2.

New York, 1929, ch. 16, sec. 353a.

North Carolina, 1929, ch. 87, secs. 4, 5.

Ohio, Gen. Code, 1926, sec. 3677.

Oregon, 1929, ch. 195, sec. 1.

Pennsylvania, 1929, ch. 318, sec. 1; ch. 446, sec. 4.

South Dakota, 1929, ch. 71, sec. 3.

Vermont, 1929, No. 60, sec. 1.

Washington, 1929, ch. 93, sec. 1.

West Virginia, 1929, ch. 61, sec. 5.

Wisconsin, 1929, ch. 348, sec. 3; ch. 521, sec. 1; Stat. 114.12.

54. See Clayton and Lambert Mfg. Co. *v.* City of Detroit, 34 Fed. (2d) 303.

The closing and relocation of highways for this purpose is specifically authorized by Conn., 1929, ch. 236; Ind., 1929, ch. 57.

55. Instances of this are:

Connecticut, 1929, ch. 281.

Kentucky, 1926, ch. 107.

Rhode Island, 1929, ch. 1353.

See U. S. Res. of Mar. 4, 1929, ch. 713, 45 Stat. 1698.

56. An instance of this is Kentucky, 1926, ch. 107.

57. California has passed a statute (1929, ch. 847) providing for the formation of airport districts on petition of a percentage of the voters of the proposed district, with power to sell bonds, levy taxes, etc.

58. The decisions are conflicting, but this seems to be the prevailing law. McQuillan, "Municipal Corporations," 2d ed. (1927), secs. 1210, 1215.

In the case of airports condemnation outside municipal limits was upheld under general laws in City of Spokane *v.* Williams, reported in *U. S. Daily,* June 17, 1930.

59. Arkansas, 1929, No. 135, sec. 4.

Idaho, 1929, ch. 106.

Oklahoma, 1929, ch. 83.

60. Arkansas, 1929, No. 135, sec. 4.

Indiana, 1927, p. 160, sec. 3838 (5917, vol. 1).

Kansas, 1929, ch. 5, sec. 3.

Massachusetts, 1928, ch. 350, sec. 1.

Michigan, 1929, No. 103, sec. 6; No. 210, sec. 3.

Mississippi, 1929, ch. 63, sec. 3.

New Hampshire, 1929, ch. 90, sec. 1.

New Jersey, 1929, ch. 350, secs. 1, 2.

New York, 1929, ch. 16, sec. 353a.

North Carolina, 1929, ch. 87, sec. 4.

Oregon, 1929, ch. 195, sec. 1.

Pennsylvania, 1929, ch. 318, sec. 1; ch. 446, sec. 4.

Vermont, 1929, No. 60, sec. 1.

West Virginia, 1929, ch. 61, sec. 5.

Wisconsin, 1929, ch. 521, sec. 1.

61. Illinois, 1929, p. 590, sec. 1.

Iowa, 1929, ch. 133.

Michigan, 1929, No. 193, sec. 1.

Missouri, 1929, p. 345, sec. 2.

Wisconsin, 1929, ch. 201, sec. 1.

62. See Nichols, "Eminent Domain," 2d ed. (1917), pp. 972, 995; Lewis, "Eminent Domain," 2d ed. (1900), p. 345, sec. 140, note 51, *et seq.;* Corpus Juris, "Eminent Domain," vol. 20, p. 598, note 76, and p. 599, note 77; McQuillan, "Municipal Corporations," 2d ed. (1927), secs. 1643, 1644, 1649.

63. City of Wichita *v.* Clapp, 125 Kansas, 100.

64. The following statutes relate to airports in parks or under park management:

California, 1927, ch. 267, p. 484, sec. 1.

Illinois, 1927, p. 616; 1929, p. 557, sec. 1.

Kansas, 1929, ch. 5, sec. 2.

Kentucky, 1928, ch. 78.

Massachusetts, 1928, ch. 388, sec. 56.

Minnesota, 1927, ch. 62, sec. 1625–5; 1929, ch. 125, sec. 9.

Oregon, 1921, ch. 45, sec. 9.

Wisconsin, 1927, ch. 248, sec. 2705.

65. States authorizing such zoning are:

Florida, Special Acts, 1923, ch. 9915 (No. 797), p. 2690, secs. 1, 4 (applicable only to St. Petersburg).

Kentucky, 1928, ch. 80 (2d class cities).

66. Idaho, ch. 137, sec. 2 (h).

Iowa, 1929, ch. 138, sec. 6.

Michigan, 1929, No. 177.

Pennsylvania, 1927, No. 250; 1929, Nos. 175, 316, Art. II.

Virginia, 1928, Title 33A, ch. 146A.

See Connecticut, 1929, ch. 253.

Maryland, 1929, sec. 20.

67. McQuillan, "Municipal Corporations," 2d ed. (1927), sec. 1264. Property used for revenue is often held liable to tax. *Ibid.*

68. Florida, 1929, S. J. R. 89.

Georgia, 1927, p. 779, secs. 4B, 4C.

Idaho, 1929, ch. 283, sec. 4.

Indiana, 1923, ch. 182, sec. 5.

Michigan, 1929, No. 157, sec. 1.

Vermont, 1929, No. 20, sec. 1.

69. City of Mobile *v.* Lartigue, 127 So. Rep. 257 (Ala.).

70. Iowa, 1929, ch. 138, sec. 9.

South Carolina, 1929, No. 562, sec. 2.

Texas, 1929 (first session), ch. 83, sec. 3; ch. 281, sec. 3.

Wisconsin, 1929, ch. 464, sec. 1.

71. Pollock, "Torts," 11th ed. (1920), p. 451.

72. For an exhaustive discussion of the doctrine, see the article on negligence, 45 Corpus Juris, 1193, *et seq.* The applicability of the doctrine to the airplane is considered in "Transportation by air and the doctrine of *Res Ipsa Loquitur*," by William M. Allen, in the *American Bar Association Journal* for July 1, 1930.

73. Arizona, 1929, ch. 38.

Connecticut, 1929, ch. 57.

Pennsylvania, 1929, No. 317.

74. Delaware, 1923, ch. 199.

Hawaii, 1923, L. 1923, ch. 109; Rev. L. 1925, secs. 3891–3905.

Idaho, 1925, ch. 92.

Indiana, 1927, ch. 43.

Maryland, 1927, ch. 637.

Michigan, 1923, No. 224.

Minnesota, 1929, ch. 219.

Nevada, 1923, ch. 66.

New Jersey, 1929, ch. 311.

North Carolina, 1929, ch. 190.
North Dakota, 1923, ch. 1.
Rhode Island, 1929, ch. 1435.
South Carolina, 1929, ch. 189.
South Dakota, 1925, ch. 6.

Tennessee, 1923, ch. 30.
Utah, 1923, ch. 24.
Vermont, 1923, No. 155.
Wisconsin, Stat. 11405.

In Idaho (1929, ch. 88) persons engaged in aviation are exempted from the Workmen's Compensation Law.

75. California, 1929, ch. 193, sec. 394, (18).
Idaho, 1929, ch. 88.
Iowa, 1929, ch. 229, sec. 1.
Louisiana, 1926, No. 52.
Massachusetts, Gen. Laws, ch. 175, sec. 47; 1928, ch. 106, sec. 1.

Michigan, 1929, No. 154.
Ohio, 1929, p. 54, being an amendment of Gen. Code, sec. 9556.
Virginia, Corp. Com. Reg., 1929, Rule 33, given in 1929 U. S. Av. Rep. 855, *et seq.*

76. In this connection see Law *et al.*, Spartanburg County Board *v.* City of Spartanburg, 148 S. C. 229.

77. Such ordinances have been passed; see Alameda, Calif., Ordinance No. 203, Dec. 3, 1928.

Oakland, Calif., Port Ordinance No. 45, Jan. 7, 1929. Akron, O., Ordinance No. 600, June 18, 1929.

In this connection should be noted the decision of the Supreme Court of Indiana in an appeal by the General Outdoor Advertising Company against the Indianapolis Park Board, digested in *U. S. Daily* for June 29, 1930. This decision sustained the power of Indiana cities to prohibit by ordinance the erection and maintenance of advertising billboards on private property within 500 feet of the city's parks or boulevards, refusing to follow cases to the contrary in Massachusetts in 1905, in Illinois in 1911, and in Missouri and Ohio in 1912. The decision points out that since these cases were decided, stringent city planning and zoning laws have very generally in this country been passed and upheld by the courts.

The court intimates, however, that unless it can be shown that billboards already erected are a nuisance, the owners of such billboards are entitled to compensation for them if they are ordered removed.

78. Regulation of this sort by the Board of Aviation Commissioners is authorized by Indiana, 1929, ch. 171, sec. 5 (8), 9, 11.

The statute also makes subdivision within six hundred feet of an airport subject to the permission of the Board. It would be difficult to defend any action of the Board in this connection in the special interest of aviation; and there is nothing in the statute suggesting such action on their part. In any event it would seem to be the better policy to have all subdivisions controlled by the same authority.

79. Seaplane moored in navigable waters has been held to be a vessel (Reinhardt *v.* Newport Flying Service Corp., 232, N. Y. 115; see People *ex rel.* Cushing *v.* Smith, (N. Y.) 119 Misc. 294, 196 N. Y. S. 241, 206 App. Div. 642, 198 N. Y. S. 940, 206 App. Div. 726, 199 N. Y. S. 942, Laws N. Y. 1929, ch. 187).

The laws of many of the states provide that a seaplane when operated on or immediately above the water is governed by the rules regulating water navigation.

Arizona, 1929, ch. 38, sec. 7.
Delaware, 1923, ch. 199, sec. 1.
Hawaii, 1923, ch. 109, sec. 1.
Idaho, 1925, ch. 92, sec. 1.
Indiana, 1927, ch. 43, sec. 1.
Maryland, 1927, ch. 337, sec. 1.
Michigan, 1929, No. 224, sec. 1.
Missouri, 1929, p. 122, sec. 1.
Minnesota, 1929, ch. 219, sec. 1.
Nevada, 1923, ch. 66, sec. 1.

North Carolina, 1929, ch. 190, sec. 1.
North Dakota, 1923, ch. 1, sec. 1.
Rhode Island, 1929, ch. 1435, sec. 1.
South Carolina, 1929, Act 189, sec. 1.
South Dakota, 1923, ch. 6, sec. 1.
Tennessee, 1923, ch. 30, sec. 1.
Utah, 1923, ch. 24, sec. 1.
Vermont, 1923, ch. 155, sec. 1.

Many of the regulations with regard to vessels are not suitable for seaplanes; see Legislative History of Air Commerce Act of 1926, compiled by Frederick E. Lee (to be found in 1929 U. S. Av. Rep., p. 117), sec. 7 (A). Accordingly the earlier rules have been changed by the U. S. Commerce Act 1926 (Act of May 20, 1926, ch. 344, 44 Stat. L. 568), sec. 7, and the Air Commerce Regulations 1928, secs. 22 and 74 (J), so as to apply to seaplanes only in certain cases.

80. Connecticut, 1929, ch. 236, secs. 4, 5.
Indiana, 1929, ch. 171, sec. 5 (8).
New Hampshire, 1929, ch. 90, sec.

68*d* (Pub. Laws, ch. 42, sec. 68*d*).
South Carolina, 1929, No. 440.
Tennessee, Private Acts, 1929, ch. 408.

81. See Nichols, "Eminent Domain," 2d ed. (1917), sec. 49.
82. See generally, article on "Adjoining Landowners," in 1 Corpus Juris, p. 1230, note 95.
83. State *ex rel.* Mitchell *v.* Coffeeville, 127 Kansas, 663.

84. California, 1927, ch. 267, p. 485, sec. 4.
Indiana, 1921, ch. 111, sec. 1; 1929, ch. 57, sec. 5 (5).
Iowa, 1929, ch. 138, sec. 8.
Nebraska, 1929, ch. 35, sec. 5.
New Jersey, 1928, ch. 181; 1929, ch. 26.
Oklahoma, 1929, ch. 11, sec. 1.

Pennsylvania, 1923, No. 191, sec. 460*a*-3; 1923, No. 192, sec. 460*b*-3; 1927, ch. 494, sec. 3.
Rhode Island, 1929, ch. 1353, sec. 5.
Wisconsin, 1927, ch. 248 (27.05), sec. (4).
Wyoming, 1929, ch. 66, sec. 4.
See Idaho, 1929, ch. 106, sec. 1.

POSTSCRIPT

The Cleveland Airport Decision. Since this report was written, an important case (Swetland *v.* Curtiss Airports Corporation), long pending, has been decided in the United States District Court (Northern District of Ohio, Eastern Division, July 7, 1930, Hahn, Judge) [1] in conformity, in so far as involved in the case, with the conclusions of law as stated in the report.

[1] Subsequently, in August, 1930, clarified by minor changes and additions, and here summarized in the light of these changes.

The action was for injunction for trespass and the maintenance of a nuisance. The plaintiffs are the owners of a highly improved country estate, in a sparsely settled neighborhood near Cleveland. The defendants are the owners of an airport adjacent to it. The field is well equipped and conducted. In taking off and landing the defendants traverse the air space less than 500 feet above plaintiff's land, and subsequently, the air space at a greater altitude above it.

The Court holds that

1. A private airport and flying school is not a nuisance *per se*, but may be a nuisance if improperly located or conducted. The present field is properly located, and in the main properly conducted.

2. Flight, in this locality, above five hundred feet is not a trespass since this air space is not owned by the plaintiffs. As conducted it was not a nuisance. The state laws, together with the United States laws and regulations allowing such flights, were valid police legislation.

3. Flight at less than 500 feet over plaintiff's land is a trespass and will be enjoined. The existing laws and regulations do not attempt to legalize them as against the owner of the land underneath. "Until the progress of aerial navigation has reached a point of development where airplanes can readily reach an altitude of 500 feet before crossing the property of an adjoining owner, where such crossing involves an unreasonable interference with property rights or with effective possession, owners of airports must acquire landing fields of sufficient area to accomplish that result. In such instances to fly over the lands of an adjoining owner at lower altitudes, the owners of airports must secure the consent of adjoining property owners, or acquire such rights by condemnation when appropriate enabling statutes are enacted. Smith *v.* New England Aircraft Co., Inc., (Mass.) 170 N. E. R. 385, 391, 393. (See an able article by Charles P. Hine, of Counsel in this case, 'Home *Versus* Aeroplane,' *American Bar Association Journal*, April, 1930.)

" Whether property rights or effective possession is interfered with unreasonably is a question of fact in the particular case . . . .

"It is of course conceivable and very probable that in other cases, depending upon the character and extent of the operations of the adjoining airport, effective possession may not be interfered with by flights at lesser altitudes than 500 feet in taking off and landing."

SUBJECT INDEX [1]

[1] Only cities mentioned in the main text are included in this Index. Other cities will be found in footnotes and in the alphabetical lists and tables in the Appendices.